ATTRACT

IT

ATTRACT
IT

Beyond Positive Thinking

■ Health ■ Professional & Business Success
■ Financial Freedom ■ Love ■ Healthy Weight
■ Happy Independent Aging
■ Dream Job ■ Positive Organizational Development

The Natural Law of Attraction:
THE OWNER'S MANUAL
Be, Do & Have More of Whatever YOU Want.

Gisèle Guénard *BScN, Master of Education*

ENERGIZE IT ! Book Gisèle for
your event !
www.visionarease.com

iUniverse, Inc.
New York Lincoln Shanghai

Attract It
Beyond Positive Thinking

iUniverse books may be ordered through booksellers or by contacting:

iUniverse
2021 Pine Lake Road, Suite 100
Lincoln, NE 68512
www.iuniverse.com
1-800-Authors (1-800-288-4677)

Because of the dynamic nature of the Internet, any Web addresses or links contained in this book may have changed since publication and may no longer be valid.

ISBN: 978-0-595-43377-3 (pbk)
ISBN: 978-0-595-68933-0 (cloth)
ISBN: 978-0-595-87704-1 (ebk)

Printed in the United States of America

No celebrities or other authors were interviewed for this book. The information contained is based on the opinion of the author. Other persons may have differing opinions. Any products, company names, or/and other commercial terms, are used as information for the reader. The author has no known connection to any of these. This book is for information, and intended to add to the body of materials in the schools of thought known as success strategy and positive thinking. It is not to be used as a substitute for medical or business advice or consultation from any licensed health care provider or business consultant. The reader should consult their health care provider before starting any exercise program. The author and publisher expressly disclaim responsibility for any adverse effects arising from the use or application of any of the information contained in this book.

First Edition

~ ~

For Holly and Sarah, who inspire me with joy.
And for John, the love of my life.

~ ~

Without the love and teachings of my very special mother, Yvonne, I would not be where I am today. A series of events presented themselves in my life around the time of her death on September 26, 2006. These events led me to the writing of this book.

Yvonne lived the natural law of Attraction. For her, the glass was always half full, until the day she died in her sleep, *as she intended*, at the age of 94. Against all odds … adversity, war, poverty, illness, widowhood, the death of her beloved firstborn son, and most of her eleven siblings, as well as the isolation of total blindness, Yvonne smiled, kept up a "chipper" outlook, and even in her final days, reminded us all that …

"For goodness sakes, there is always
something to look forward to."

Yvonne 1946

Thank you Mum. Until we meet again …

Acknowledgement

To the following people, I express my greatest appreciation for their support during the writing of this book:

~ My wonderful husband John, for his rock-solid faith in me
~ My very special daughters, Holly & Sarah, for their cheerleading and opinions
~ The very special friends who shared their stories for this book
~ My good friend Norm, for his profound understanding of the meaning of this work
~ My professional friends and colleagues, for their respect and encouragement
~ To iUniverse, for their professional guidance and for enabling me to *"say the words"*
~ To Nancy Genesse, for her photographic artistry

To the five who are always there for me, from the other side … *à la prochaine* … until the next time.

Contents

Preface

Do good things with what you know.
Gisèle Guénard

Blessed with many gifts and skills, I have strived to live by this concept.

~ ~

Wonderful opportunities have presented themselves throughout my life, causing some to think I simply "got lucky". On the contrary, I have faced many difficult challenges. Yet powerful, natural forces are at work in my life and in yours, bringing us both to exactly where we are right now. We all have access to the key that releases these forces. We can all make a difference in our own and in the lives of those around us by guiding ourselves towards the manifestation of what is good and what is right. This is true in our personal lives, in our work and in our organizations.

My story, some of which is woven through this book, is that of countless others, who chose to travel paths their parents and grandparents never dreamed possible … by changing the way we *think*.

We all make mistakes and bad decisions. However, by striving to do good with our own unique accumulation of knowledge, positive events will eventually manifest. Though some may be misguided and choose to take the wrong path once in the possession of all manner of knowledge, know that the efforts of those who *do good things with what we know* will always prevail. Just *think* of the possibilities …

Introduction

How This "Owner's Manual" Can Help You Have *More* of What You Want

What does it cost to own the keys to being, doing, and having more of absolutely anything you want … anything you put your mind to? Nothing. All the keys you need are in your hands, and more importantly … between your ears. *You simply need to learn how to use what you already posess.*

Chapters 1 & 2

Revealed here are the keys, or "the strangest secret", as Earl Nightingale so clearly stated in 1956, which you need to achieve every goal you can think of … every one … or something better. This material serves as the foundation of knowledge you need to create a better future … the future you want.

Chapters 3 to 8

In these sections, you will learn a simple and unique 2-step system to take you Beyond Positive Thinking, and beyond a simple introduction to the law of Attraction. You will enjoy venturing beyond the theory, as well as the ideas and concepts presented in other books and materials, and learn *how to actually "do" the attracting.* Anyone can use this system and the easy, yet powerful Exercises designed for *you* to attract *your* desires.

Questions & Answers

These questions are among the most common for anyone exploring how they can apply strategies beyond positive thinking, including the keys of Attraction, in their own lives.

The Natural Law of Attraction: The Manual is Here

Italics, capitalization and other non-traditional forms of writing and writing style are used occasionally, to highlight key points, and to help you embed powerful concepts into your way of thinking. It can literally change your life, as it has for countless others.

Written in a style intended to provide you with a relaxing and enjoyable learning experience, *Attract It: Beyond Positive Thinking* is an "owner's manual" to help you learn *how* to apply these wonderful concepts … *how* to turn the keys.

Whether you are seeking to improve the quality of your personal life, to catapult your business to success, or to apply the concepts of Attraction to your organization's development, you will benefit most by approaching the book in this manner:

1. Enjoy a complete first reading, pencil in hand, and think of the book as a discovery tool. You are encouraged to scribble, make notes and circle points of interest as you initially read the book, from cover to cover.

2. Try each Exercise at least once as you read the Chapters.

3. Continue to review and even re-read the book to incorporate the strategies into your day-to-day life.

4. Use, re-use and adapt the Exercises as tools to improve your life by attracting *more of what you want* and *less of what you do not want*.

5. Visit the youattractnow.com web site to learn more.

Terms and Symbols

You will see the term "Law Of Attraction" also termed "LOA", simplified to "Attraction", just as the "Law Of Gravity" is known as simply "Gravity". Some teachers use the term "scientific law of Attraction". "*Natural* law of Attraction" is the term I use and teach, reflecting my personal interpretation. All these terms are correct.

    ⚷ The Key symbol highlights points, which you will want to begin to integrate as soon as possible.

BA: The "BA" acronym stands for Business Application. Whether you are a new entrepreneur, in a leadership role, or part of a team, the BA notes will be useful to you in your work life.

Enjoy!

Chapter 1

This Is *It*

There *Is* A Way

Decide to apply the information presented within the pages of this book, and your life will undergo positive transformation. Whether your wish is to improve yourself, your business, or the organization you are a part of, the principles are the same. If this information is new to you, and you choose to apply it, then you are about to begin a life-changing journey many have taken before. On this journey, people find something all of us seek … *the power to be, have and do much, much more of what they truly want, and even … exactly what they want.* You will learn to easily apply the power of Attraction to transform your life. Around the world, more and more people are learning that the law of Attraction is in fact, one of the great natural laws governing our existence. Beyond the theory, the simple "how to" system presented here will show you the way

No one person or group is responsible for inventing or discovering the natural law of Attraction. It has been spoken of, or written about, for millennia. Those of us who are teaching or coaching success strategies, positive thinking and the elements of the law of Attraction are simply guides, or mentors. Individuals and organizations the world over are seeking a method to deliberately improve their circumstances. This book presents that method to you in a way you can easily apply.

How much transformation and positive change you create by using the strategies in this book is up to you. You may have massive and positive change in your life, or you may choose to simply dabble in the techniques and gradually improve your situation.

How do successful people "do it"? What are *they* doing that is different? How do *they* attract what they want? How do *they* get all the breaks? Successful people do it like this: *They are "doing" a few simple things, repeatedly.*

Is This a "Spiritual", "Religious" or "New Age" Thing?

On the contrary. It is at work *now*, in everyone's life. It is simply one of the laws of nature. You can look at it as a healthy way of thinking, good business, or a spiritual way … that is up to you. Whether you are agnostic, atheist, or belong to organized religion, rest assured that in every successful way of life, every religion, and in every philosophy handed down since the beginning of time, the concepts within this book are found there as well. *The law of Attraction is working now, for everybody, all the time.* What is missing is the "how". Should you wish to more deliberately apply the concepts of Attraction in your own spiritual life, you will find them easy to incorporate into your regular practices. Should you wish to use your own terminology, and call "Attraction" something else, or a name that matches your own spiritual or religious beliefs, you are free to do so, and the wonderful results will be the same ... if you follow the process.

Psychology 101

Many Psychologists and other professionals working in the field of mental health incorporate the techniques of positive thinking and re-framing into their practices. They regularly assist the client to focus on what they do want as opposed to the endless fixation on the depressing trigger events the client sees as the reason for their current state. There is no question that these techniques, incorporated into standard health counseling, are effective. The professionals may not be using the same terminology, but the most successful among them all enable the client to move in a more positive direction, attracting better and healthier outcomes by changing the way they think.

Much controversy exists around any massive, popular representation of knowledge previously held and used by a select few. The increased awareness around Attraction, this most important universal law, is no different. Some psychologists are concerned about people now believing they can magically make things appear simply by imagining or visualizing those things. This concern is well founded, and in fact, this book teaches the things *you must do*, and the *changes you must make* to create a better life for yourself.

Quest

Humankind has always searched for "ways", or what were thought to be "secrets" of success, sometimes consciously, though not always. I have always had some level of awareness that the natural law of Attraction existed, and have applied elements of it for the continuous improvement of my own experience. Reading Joseph Murphy's classic "The Power of Your Subconscious Mind" was my introduction to the law of Attraction. I read my now dog-eared copy several times, each time learning new information that helped in my parenting, my career and business ventures, and all aspects of my personal life.

I learned that the key to attracting our desires is this:

$$\frac{\text{Decide} + \text{Energize}}{\textit{Know}} = \text{Attraction}$$

I learned that each one of us can:

- ✓ Find a way to significantly contribute to saving our environment
- ✓ Enjoy Financial Freedom
- ✓ Find True and Lasting Love
- ✓ Do Good in the World
- ✓ Lose Weight & Keep It Off
- ✓ Be Part of The Solution
- ✓ Be Healthy
- ✓ Discover & Invent New Things to Help Others
- ✓ Land Our Dream Job
- ✓ Build a Successful Businesses or Organization
- ✓ Travel
- ✓ Climb Mount Everest
- ✓ Uncover and Develop Our Physical Beauty
- ✓ Paint Photograph Sculpt Write Sing ... and Get Paid For It
- ✓ Teach What We Know
- ✓ Sing Model Act
- ✓ Move to the Country
- ✓ Live by the Water
- ✓ And So On ...

What are *your* desires? You can attract them into your life now.

Introduce Yourself to the Natural Law of Attraction

It has been around forever ...

When the Student is Ready, the Teacher Appears

My first memory of knowing that somehow, the *capacity to think purposefully* was a powerful and exciting feature of *who I was*, occurs at the age of eight. As my Mother and I were doing the dishes in front of the kitchen window one evening, I distinctly remember telling her, that I had been having a wonderful time *thinking, just thinking ...* all by myself in my room, thinking about all kinds of wonderful things I could do.

At sixteen, I began post-secondary studies, and was introduced to "success" concepts. In some way, I knew these concepts would help me enjoy the life I wanted. Some of these concepts or ideas had elements I now know as the natural law of Attraction. Some of them were taught in science courses, some in psychology classes and some in professional level health care studies. I remember one course in particular, called The World's Living Religions. Born and raised a Catholic, I knew very little about any other faith. I was fascinated to learn, that all religions had a lot in common. They all held some sort of "*Ask and You Shall Receive*" dogma, or belief.

For the past 20 years, I have been studying the elements of the natural law of Attraction in a more focused manner. The terminology has varied, depending on the writer. I have read, listened to and viewed, as well as practiced, ideas from the teachings of Behrend, Patterson, Peale, Hill, Dyer, James, Ponder, Chopra, and many more. Most recently, Rhonda Byrne and others have brought worldwide attention to this subject. I experienced a profound understanding of the concept *"we attract what we think about"*, many years ago, when I first heard Earl Nightingale's classic recording of "The Strangest Secret". As I studied, I came to realize … *its All The Same Thing!* <u>Decide + Energize/*Know* = Attraction!</u>

Why present this information then, if others have already done so? This information is so vital, so transformative, that those who have the skills to do so simply must share the keys to its application. There is a thirst for this knowledge in every country, in every society, in every home and organization. It will take many teachers, with a myriad of approaches, and from every background, to move this information throughout the world. If you are a "ready student", I hope I can be of service to you by sharing my unique teaching approach.

The approach I present is fresh and unique in its simplicity, while being supported by a solid base of knowledge and true-life examples. My approach is applicable to all situations, be they personal or professional. Compare this to music in various settings, styles and cultures. The basic elements of music are identical regardless of the style. Many types of music teachers and methods, as well as countless instruments, exist however, appealing to every type of person or group. Some may prefer the spiritual nature of certain approaches to teaching law of Attraction. Others may gravitate to a more business-like approach, or even a psychology slant. Some prefer to access the keys from female teachers, some from male role models. Certain individuals will enjoy a light-hearted humorous approach, while others prefer a philosophical style of presentation. The basic keys to attracting success in any endeavor, simplified and combined with effective learning exercises, will provide you with exactly what you require to have more of what you truly want.

How Did It All Get So Complicated?

It really is *not* complicated. It really *is very* simple.

For some of you, this natural law of Attraction "stuff", also known as "LOA", for "Law Of Attraction", is brand new. For others, some of what you will read in the first two chapters of this book will be familiar. It has been written about in the actual terms of "law of Attraction" since the turn of the last century. The basic principles have been written about by for centuries, in varying and often complex terms. In one form of another, for over thousands of years, the law of Attraction has been clearly understood and deliberately practiced, though kept secret by most of the few who truly understood it.

Once your interest for information about Attraction is piqued, the desire to know more may be continually and delightfully present in your life.

Have you ever stumbled across a method for improving your life, for attracting things to you, known that it made sense and "should" work, yet you just could not follow the "plan", or the "way" as outlined? Certain methods obviously work for the person promoting it, as well as for other people. Then why is everybody not using the same method? Why isn't the whole world a better place because of it? One reason is that many methods promoted are complex systems requiring study, time, expensive tools and aids, attending meetings and so on. These effective, yet complex, methods for improving your life *are* unquestionably based on the law of Attraction. It is a great thing that many wise practitioners have written about these concepts and created systems to help others. There is however, an easier way to apply the law of Attraction.

Are you starting to feel a twinge of excitement? Hang on to that thought. That thought, or feeling is part of the law of Attraction at work now, and ... you are *already* experiencing its benefits.

Proof/Evidence

Acknowledging proof, or *evidence,* of the law of Attraction, is part of how it actually works. Throughout this book, you will find Proof Notes ... factual accounts experienced by myself, and others who graciously shared their examples for this book. More importantly, you will soon begin to acknowledge your own proof ... *and watch what happens then!*

People everywhere, from all walks of life, have followed paths similar to mine, since the beginning of time. My story pales by comparison to the trials and hardships of many great women and men, whom we hold up as examples of success, despite seemingly impossible circumstances. Among them are Helen Keller, Nelson Mandela, and Mother Theresa. I encourage you to read and learn about these wonderful people, and see for yourself the common thread woven through all their stories.

Elements of the Law of Attraction at Work in Our Family

I was born during the Baby Boom, into a rather ordinary rural Canadian family. By the time I was seven, my father, a WW2 veteran, had had several spinal fusions and would never be able to return to his underground mining job. We never felt "poor". However, by many people's standards, we certainly were. Though they were well read and respected, my parents never went to high school. Somehow, I experienced the *contrast* of going from these humble beginnings, to providing leadership as the CEO of a busy hospital. How did this happen?

As you saw in the Acknowlegment at the start of this book, my Mother has been my inspiration. She unknowingly modeled the natural law of Attraction, inspiring and encouraging me. What follows here are four examples of how she applied the power of Attraction in her day-to-day life. (Note: the Italics are used in this section to highlight key Attraction elements at play)

1. *Attracting* a Cottage

My mother, Yvonne, was the nanny for a wealthy merchant family. She spent summers with them at their vacation home, on Lake Huron's beautiful Manitoulin Island. This was in the 30's and 40's when single women did not buy property, let alone build their own leisure homes. Spending her time being in the beautiful surroundings of the family's summer estate burned a *desire* into Yvonne's brain. She *decided* she would have her own summer place one day. *Constantly dreaming* about her little cottage by the lake, yet still single and approaching 40, she managed to purchase a beautiful peninsula on the lake close to where she grew up, north of the historic French River. She longed for and *desired* a log cabin cottage with a stone fireplace. Sure enough, the log cabin *manifested*, with the help of her brothers, complete with stone fireplace. Over 50 years old now, it stands today, a monument to her spirit, and a perfect example of the law of Attraction.

2. *Deliberate Attraction*

Yvonne was a devout Catholic and framed her life and her successes in the terms of a Christian, and a loving belief in God. She found great joy in her faith. It *energized* her. If times were tough, she prayed even harder … fervent, *positive prayer* … for a solution to whatever the problem was. She *was constantly creating pictures in her mind*, and *intending* what she wanted. She *knew* there would be an answer. She was in fact, *deliberately attracting or creating* her future, rather than Attracting by "default".

Solutions came to her in many forms—the energy to spring into action, ways to stretch the family income, unexpected resources and new ideas. Even in the leanest of times, Mum and Dad put delicious food on the table, and made sure we got to the dentist and took our vitamins.

3. *Think* of a Way

Mum taught me that when faced with challenges, "*You put your thinking cap on*", because there is always "*something you can do*". Many families would have fallen apart, faced with some of our challenges. At one point, in the early 1960's, before the days of "workmen's compensation", my Dad was in a back brace recuperating from yet another spinal fusion. Mum had no intention of letting this setback bring us down. Her *intention* was of a different sort indeed. She sprang into action. After all, they had three children under the age of 10 to look after! She got into the blue Volkswagen™ (my Dad was a VW™ fan—we had 9 "bugs" in a row) and went door to door selling Watkins™ products while my Dad learned new skills. Women in our rural area did not "have jobs". We went with her, three little kids on an adventure. *She made it fun.* I can still hear her grinding the standard transmission on the Beetle. And, oh—a driver's license? For goodness sakes, she did not need one of those! By the way, she was no twenty-something mom. Single until the age of 41, she did not start her family until her mid-forties. What gave her the drive, the ambition, the energy?

4. *Attracting the Ultimate*: The Pacemaker Story

My favorite example of the power of Attraction at work for my Mother is the following. All her life, she *prayed* that she would "die in her sleep", a common desire for all of humankind. Dying in one's sleep sure beats all the other painful options. Yvonne, however, gave this *wish* of hers quite a bit of *focus*.

She had begun having "spells" in her seventies. We found her blue and unconscious on more than one occasion. One day, well into her 80's, she had another episode. I found her unconscious in her room. She subsequently had cardiac testing and was found to have a serious heart condition. In the Cardiologist's office, she learned of the ominous "heart block" lurking in her chest. The Doctor told her she needed a pacemaker, while he whispered to me that she might have a year or so to live. After **hearing** about the procedure, which was *not* what she wanted (*contrast*), she **asked**, "*Well, what will happen if I don't take the pacemaker?*" "You will fall asleep **and** not wake up!" the Doctor told her. "*Perfect! That's what I have always prayed for!*" (*Deciding what she did want*) was her answer to *that!* And home we **went. She** died on September 26, 2006, at the age of 94, in her sleep, just as she **had** hoped, prayed and wished for. (*Proof of the ultimate kind*)

Mum taught me to *Decide* what I wanted, and "*get on with it*". She never used the terms "Decide Energize *Know*", or "law of Attraction", yet she lived it in a million ways.

Deliberate Attraction

Who you are is irrelevant. *What* you did before now is irrelevant. *When* you Decide to begin deliberately applying Attraction to your life is up to you. *Where* you are now is irrelevant. The fact that you are reading this book now is proof of the law of Attraction. *How?*

1. At some point, you began seeking ... asking ... deciding ... wishing ... *thinking* ... about finding a way to improve your life, or solve a problem.

2. A powerful force *matched your desire*, and put this information in your hands. And so, what you were asking for materialized ... in the form of this book. You *deliberately chose* to read it, therefore giving it your *attention, energy and focus*.

Why would you now want to learn about and apply Attraction? So that you can *deliberately attract what you want* instead of attracting what you do *not* want, by default.

Your Library

Whether your quest is for business success, organizational development, or personal success, after reading this book, you may want to know more about LOA, and you may wish to study the ideas and related concepts more thoroughly. I encourage you to do so. Hear and read the words of the masters, and build your own collection of inspiring information related to the law of Attraction. The following list of writers, whose works are widely available, are some of my personal favourites. Their "take", or terminology, on Attraction varies. However, the concepts are closely related or in fact, *the same*.

Joseph Murphy
Genevieve Behrend
Rhonda Byrne
William James
Catherine Ponder
Normand Vincent Peale
Napoleon Hill
Elizabeth Towne
Earl Nightingale
Deepak Chopra
Dr. Wayne Dyer

Words of wisdom from these great teachers:

"We go where our vision is." Joseph Murphy

"Try to remember that the picture you think, feel and see is reflected into the Universal Mind, and by the natural law of reciprocal action must return to you in either spiritual or physical form. Knowledge of this law of reciprocal action between the individual and the Universal Mind opens to you free access to all you may wish to possess or to be."
Genevieve Behrend

"The greatest discovery of my generation is that a human being can alter his life by altering his attitudes."
William James (*Attributed*)

"If you want greater prosperity in your life, start forming a vacuum to receive it."
Catherine Ponder

"Change your thoughts, and you change your world."
Norman Vincent Peale

"The starting point of all achievement is desire."
Napoleon Hill

"Man is a magnet, and every line and dot and detail of his experiences come by his own attraction."
Elizabeth Towne

"We become what we think about."
Earl Nightingale

"Whatever relationships you have attracted in your life at this moment, are precisely the ones you need in your life at this moment."
Deepak Chopra

"Self-worth comes from one thing—thinking that you are worthy."
Dr. Wayne Dyer

Now … *you* will learn the simplest of all methods, the Key, to begin manifesting what *you* want in *your* life.

How Do I Attract What _I_ Want?

**The key to attracting what you want,
or something better, is that
whatever you repeatedly think about,
<u>with simultaneous good feelings</u>,
will eventually come to you.**

That is It. **It is the natural law of Attraction.** It is irrefutable.
It is at work in every molecule of the universe.

In order to understand Attraction, let us study the key words in our definition.

Key Word # 1: Key

Keys start engines, unlock doors, treasure chests, and all manner of places where valuable things reside. You need a key to "get at" what is out of reach at this time. It is recommended that you listen to the famed 1956 Earl Nightingale recording "The Strangest Secret", where Earl explains the universal truth that _we can only become what we think about._ You may prefer to view the movie, "The Secret", Rhonda Byrne's masterpiece recapping the law of Attraction. It is an excellent presentation of teachings by the masters I list previously ... the same ones whose books have lined my shelves for twenty years.

The Key, or the secret, is of course, that _whatever you repeatedly think about, with simultaneous good feelings, will eventually come to you._ There is a reason for repeating this message, or definition, frequently. To change your way of thinking may seem awkward at first. Repetition of _two basic steps_ will get you there. In fact, repetition is a powerful strategy to Energize your desire and cause it to materialize.

Thinking about a thing, repeatedly, with positive feelings about it, _will cause it to manifest into your life._ It will "show up". Why is this?

Energy, Quantum Physics and You

Thoughts are things. Strange as this may sound to the uninitiated, many powerful scientific minds are now studying and concurring about this phenomenon. Quantum field theorists, working in a complex area of science, know that nothing is truly solid. Rather, *everything is energy.* Atoms are not solid at all. Particles, even smaller than atoms, are not solid either. In fact, deep underground laboratories in the growing Canadian city of Sudbury, study these infinitesimally small bodies. A mile deep in the earth, the Sudbury Neutrino Observatory (SNO Lab) is garnering worldwide attention.

What does this have to do with the natural law of Attraction? As Earl Nightingale, Catherine Ponder, and others so clearly stated, *thoughts are energy,* and *thoughts create things.* When we observe these sub-atomic particles, many now theorise that we actually somehow *cause them to appear.* Yes. That is correct. People with PhD's, and physics degree letters too numerous to fit on a business card, are studying this phenomenon right now. The tiny particles seem to appear when we give them *attention.* It seems that when no one is peering though the powerful electron microscopes, the little blips, or "neutrinos", are simply *not there.* Thinking about them, observing, and paying *attention* to them, in essence, seems to *create them.* (A "simple" interpretation of Quantum Theory is found in Dr. Deepak Chopra's fascinating writings, should this be of interest to you.)

So what? There is a natural law at work in creation, in *creating.* Deliberately focus attention on something (*thinking*) and you will create it. *It is law. It is irrefutable. It is at work in every molecule of the universe. It is the law of Attraction. People, events and things materialize by our thinking about them.* Thoughts create things!

Proof Note : The Sandwich

My daughter Holly was walking home from high school, through the city core. She was carrying a heavy backpack and in the words of every teenager, "Starving!" Having no money with her, she was approaching the Burger King™, about a block away. Smelling the burgers grilling, she started to wish that she had some money to buy a BK Chicken Sandwich™. She was *really* thinking about it, when Lo and Behold! She spotted a free coupon for a BK Chicken Sandwich™ on the pavement! She picked it up, went in to the restaurant, and thoroughly enjoyed the object of her desire.

⊶ Key Word # 2: Attracting

To attract something, put your attention on that which you want. That is how law of Attraction brings it to you. *What* you think about is irrelevant to the law of Attraction. In fact, *whether you want it or not, if you keep paying attention to it, with feeling, you will get it ... good or bad.* This explains why without LOA, it is difficult to get out of debt. Debt has become *the* biggest challenge for many well-meaning and intelligent people today, because they keep *thinking about their personal debt.* By thinking about it, while simultaneously experiencing strong (negative) feelings, they attract and maintain the problem. By learning and applying LOA, you can change your thoughts and start thinking about zero credit card balances and growing investment balances instead. *Then watch what happens.*

☯━ Key Word # 3: Want

It is OK to want things. Really. Look at any healthy, successful, or wealthy person. Look at great and influential people like Mother Teresa, Martin Luther King and Nelson Mandela, David Suzuki and even American Idol winners. They *want* to be the way they are, and do the things they are doing. They confidently talk about their desires, and give them their *attention,* their *focus* and their *energy.* By knowing *what you want* and learning to think about your desires in a powerful positive way, you will trigger the forces of Attraction to greatly improve your circumstances.

☯━ Or Something Better

You will sometimes attract something different and ultimately *better* than what you first began to focus on. You have already experienced this phenomenon many times in your life.

☯━ Key Word # 4: Whatever

What is *your* "Whatever"? What is your greatest need, want or desire right now? What are your hopes and dreams? There is no need to worry that someone else already has what you want. There is plenty of everything for everyone. People all over the world have different interests, wants and desires. You will learn to Decide what your *whatever* is, and to manifest it. You will have many *whatever's* in your life. One of them could even be to live a healthy happy 100 years and to die in your sleep.

☯━ Key Word # 5: Repeatedly

You will repeatedly think about your "*whatever's.* You will fill your mind with delightful thoughts of the things you want. Instead of a jumble of "To Do's", worries, stresses, lists and images, your mind will begin to focus more and more clearly on the things you want to manifest. This will occur by *repeating* the thought over and over again. Reading and frequently reviewing Attraction material will help. You will pick up a new, inspirational tidbit each time, even if you have read or reviewed the same material many times.

⚷ Key Word # 6: Think

It all happens in the *thinking process*. The act of thinking, with feeling, will bring the thing to you. Sometimes, you will think of a thing, with very little feeling, perhaps simply giving it a bit of attention, and it will appear. We call these "co-incidences". Thinking triggers the law of Attraction to mobilize. It also catapults you into action. You will be inspired to try new ways to solve problems. Ideas will come to you. Helpful people will show up in your life. Not-so-helpful people will fall back or even disappear. You will feel hope and excitement about the possibilities that develop on the *movie screen of your mind*. Thoughts are words, pictures, sensations and awareness that exist in your mind. *Thinking is the most powerful voluntary act humans have the ability to perform.* You will learn to build your thinking skills. And whatever you want will appear.

⚷ Key Words # 7: Simultaneous Good Feelings

These words are kept "as one" for an important reason. *While* you are thinking the thing you want, if you *feel good feelings,* the certainty and speed at which your desire will materialize are greatly increased. The better you get at thinking the thought with simultaneous good feelings, the faster you will change your entire life. It will amaze you.

⚷ Key Words # 8: Will Eventually Come To You

By deliberately using the 2-step formula, your "Whatever" *will eventually* materialize, in one form or another, sometimes precisely as you envisioned it. What you want *will* appear. Your dreams *will* become reality. "Eventually" can be a long period, or it can be shockingly fast. It all depends on how quickly you correctly apply the principles of Attraction. Remember:

> The key to attracting what you want, or something better, is that
> *whatever you repeatedly think about,*
> <u>with</u> *simultaneous good feelings, will eventually come to you.*

But Isn't It All Just Co-incidence?

No. There is no such thing as "Co-incidence". With all due respect to the "definer" of the word "co-incidence" ... whoever that was just did not know about or understand the natural law of Attraction.

Just as we once thought the earth was flat, we have erroneously thought of co-incidence as simply "interesting synchronicity", with no real significance. When people hear a story like the one about Holly's chicken sandwich, some say, "Well, those are just co-incidences!" They do not understand the significance of the fact that what they saw as "co-incidence" was something that was, in fact attracted by someone *thinking* about it. Co-incidence events are *evidence*, or *proof* that Attraction is at work. Every time you notice a co-incidence, or synchronicity, from now on, enjoy it as a little bit of proof, a gentle reminder, that Attraction is the real phenomenon at work. The evidence is irrefutable. The following Exercise will help you identify this type of evidence, present in your life.

Exercise # 1. <u>Evidence</u>	
Over the next few days, think back on 10 co-incidence examples from your own or your friends' and family's lives. Complete the following table by jotting down the thought you were having on the left side of the table. On the right, jot down the "co-incidence" that subsequently occurred. You will begin to see the fact that Attraction *is* at work in your life right now.	
Something You Were Thinking About	**The Co-Incidence That Happened**
E.g.; Someone you had not seen in 3 years	You met that person at the drug store.
1	
2	
3	
4	
5	
6	
7	
8	
9	
10	

The law of Attraction is always at work in the co-incidence phenomenon. Deliberately applying the natural law of Attraction by **Deciding** and **Energizing** while *Knowing* will enable you to create the future you want, for yourself, or for your business.

Note: The natural law of Attraction can easily be incorporated in your parenting strategies, and taught to children, enabling them to experience life with a positive healthy attitude, and even providing them with skills to create wonderful futures for themselves.

Now let us begin.

Recap Chapter 1: <u>This Is *It*</u> ⚿

⚿ There is a way to improve your life or your business: it is the natural law of Attraction, triggered by how and what you repeatedly think

⚿ Attraction works for individuals, families and organizations ... for everything and everyone

⚿ Proof is all around us. Co-incidences are really evidence of Attraction at work

⚿ Many have written about the elements of Attraction, for centuries.

⚿ The Key to attracting what you want, or something better, is that *whatever you repeatedly think about, with simultaneous good feelings, will eventually come to you.*

⚿ The formula is **Decide + Energize/*Know* = Attraction**

Questions & Ideas

Chapter 2

Healthy Thinking

A Fundamental Change

Are you sabotaging your own good intentions? You could be doing so by default. In order to *deliberately create* more of what you want in life, you need to think in a more successful manner. The creative process always requires successful thought. It can become part of who you are. In applying the law of Attraction, the ultimate creative process, "Healthy Thinking" is a fundamental change you will enjoy. It is not a 'step', but a new way of thinking ... always and from now on.

Healthy Thinking

Applying the law of Attraction to *deliberately* attract more of what you want requires you to understand and use a principle I call Healthy Thinking. You will learn to feel the difference between unhealthy thinking ... thinking that gets you nowhere, or worse, attracts negative things into you life, and Healthy Thinking. This learning will go on for some time, until you have literally changed your thinking habits, as well as your talking habits. For some, this happens quickly, for others it takes time. For some, ongoing re-visiting and re-enforcement of Healthy Thinking techniques is required for months and even years. Should you be one of those, however, who is coming from a very negative or unhealthy starting point, be encouraged and excited that your life will clearly and continuously improve as your thinking becomes healthier!

Healthy Thinking feels good. It Energizes you. It is unmistakably pleasant. It will lift your mood. It will give you hope. It will move you from the paralysis of indecision to the activity that goes along with the manifestation of your desires.

BA: Healthy Thinking can do the same for individuals or entire organizations. Successful businesses with happy satisfied clients are that way because of Healthy Thinking employees, leaders and managers.

Your Mind Plays Like a Movie

Our mind is constantly running pictures, scripts, and stories, just like a huge IMAX™ movie screen. What kind of scenes are playing on your movie screen? Are they positive, healthy, wonderful stories, places, and events that you want to move *towards*? Or are they disturbing, bleak, depressing stories and scenes that make you feel worse? Are you continuously re-living unpleasant components of your life? Are you the star of the movie scenes in your mind? Are you ensuring that the movie plots you are starring in are full of good feelings, joy, interesting events, progressive improvement and happy endings? Are you playing a successful, happy or ever-triumphant leading role in your movie?

If not, you can change these patterns, run a new movie, and transform your life to match it, by learning to apply Attraction. How?

Eliminate PW's

Healthy Thinkers use a certain type of vocabulary. This vocabulary is not only in their conversation, it is in the script of the movie playing in the mind.

BA: Successful companies teach and expect employees to use healthy, positive vocabulary in their interactions. Positive behaviour is expected of employees from the moment the client walks through the door until she or he is on their way out ... feeling good about having done business with your company. This attracts return business and better profit margins. Employees feel better about their day-to-day work interactions as well.

"PWs" are Problem Words, terms or phrases you may be using that are working just like new brakes on a car. Think of the law of Attraction as being the car, trying to get you to your destination, which is your desire. If the brakes are on, you are not going anywhere.

PW Examples:
1. Never
2. Don't
3. Hate
4. Forget it!
5. No way
6. Not
7. Swearing or cursing in frustration
8. Sarcastic 'Yeah, right!'
9. Can't
10. Won't
11. Any statement that sounds like whining

Using PWs will in fact work to attract what you *do not* want! Yikes! Just as Gravity will cause every ball thrown to eventually hit the ground, LOA simply *brings you that what you are paying attention to.* So … if you are focusing on something negative, LOA does not "know" that it is something you do not like or want. It simply brings it to you because you are giving it *attention, energy and focus.*

> Using PWs will in fact work to attract
> what you *do not* want!

Example: Sahib is constantly saying, "I hate working late!" Since his focus is on working late, and Sahib is giving it a boost of energy by expressing strong feelings about it, Attraction takes note, responds, and has no choice but to bring him lots of overtime.

Rather, Sahib should ask himself, *"What would I like instead?"* and start saying, "I love it when I get off on time!" His work stress would decrease dramatically, by virtue of the increasing frequency of going home on time.

Your mind is actually processing the PWs like a computer processes a virus, potentially crashing your dreams. And of course, viruses are contagious. People around you use PWs as well, and together, you keep the negative language pandemic going!

Feel good, knowing that when you use PWs from now on, you will recognize this, and get a tiny bit better at *not* using them next time. No one is perfect. However, everyone can develop healthier vocabulary habits. Healthy Thinking is like virus software for your brain. The information in this book will be your new virus software. Decide to catch yourself using PWs from now on, and most importantly, when you are thinking or talking about your desires, dreams and goals. Even in your thinking process, the "movie in your mind", you are using *words*. Make sure they are positive ones. Changing the way you think, and maintaining a Healthy Thinking process is a new lifelong habit, which will serve you, your family or your organization very well indeed.

How to Stop Using PWs: NLP

At one point in my life, I was newly single and raising two children on my own. I was a junior College Professor, teaching nursing, after having put myself through university by working weekends as a Registered Nurse. Being a "goal setter" since childhood, I knew that I needed a second income to give my daughters the extras that would feed their minds and help them develop to their interests. A nice neighbourhood, music lessons, and organized sports were not in our budget without extra income. Though we could barely afford it, we moved to a lovely neighbourhood in the popular hospital area of our city, with lots of girls for them to play with.

In order to achieve my financial goals, I as well as many of my friends and family, had tried a variety of home based businesses to create the second income we needed. This would create more precious time at home with my girls. From writing contracts, to sales, to singing at church weddings, you name it … I did it. Through one of these business ventures, I met a couple who told me about "NLP", or Neuro Linguistic Programming. This couple was quite successful in their home-based business and I admired their positive attitude. All manner of neat things continually happened to this couple. Now, I had not only studied and thoroughly enjoyed Psychology in university, but I was now teaching basic psychology and mental health courses to nursing students, yet I had never even heard of "NLP".

If you look up "Neuro Linguistic Programming", you will find definitions, which include elements like these:

- set of skills and techniques
- founded by John Grinder and Richard Bandler in 1975.
- patterns are created by the interactions between the brain (neuro), language (linguistic), and the body
- patterns produce both effective and ineffective behaviour

Though many academics dispute that NLP is valid in any way, all I knew at the time was that my friends were using it and, "Hey! It worked for them!" They used positive terminology most of the time. Instead of saying: "I can't afford that restaurant this week." they might say, "I love the steak at that restaurant. Let's go there next week." Lively, fun discussion would then ensue, and a different restaurant would be chosen. Another example was their avoidance of the word "No". Instead of saying "No", they would say, "I'll take XYZ instead, thank you." So used to avoiding PWs, they were no longer aware of their choice of positive vocabulary.

This "NLP idea" struck a chord with me, and I started using it with my children. I tried to make conversations positive and fun, and sometimes answered their requests with an NLP answer. Here is an example:

<u>Sarah</u>: "Mom, can I go to the store alone ... *I'm old enough ...!?*"
<u>Me</u>: "Yes ... of course ... later. I can hardly wait for you to go the store alone! In fact, I'll help you get your license when you're 16, and you can do *all* the grocery shopping. Isn't that exciting??!"

And that is exactly what happened. Sarah started imagining herself driving, and giving that idea a lot of attention, energy and focus. Sure enough, from the age of 16 on, she was our family shopper, off to the grocery store in Mom's car.

How do you get rid of your PWs? Practice. Practice. Practice. The following Exercises will kick-start you in the right direction, helping you eliminate Problem Words.

Exercise # 2. <u>Instead of Saying</u>	
Instead of Saying or Thinking:	**Practice Saying Things Like:**
"I don't have enough money."	"I'm in the process of attracting more money."
"I'm in debt up to my ears."	"I love the idea of having a zero balance on all my credit cards."
"I want to buy a car, but I can't afford it."	"My next car will be so much fun to drive. I'll be getting it in the near future."

Exercise # 3. <u>PW Fix</u>	
Ask a friend, child or spouse, to point out to you any PWs <u>you</u> frequently use. Alternatively, you can do this exercise yourself.	
Problem Word of Phrase you frequently use:	**Better, "Positive" Way to Say It:**
1	
2	
3	
4	
5	
6	
7	
8	
9	
10	

Congratulations! You have begun changing the very way you think. You are now ready to apply a simple 2-step process to enable Attraction to bring you much more of what you *truly* want.

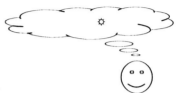

Recap Chapter 2: <u>Healthy Thinking</u>

- ⚷ In applying the law of Attraction, the *preparing* is *Healthy Thinking*. It is not a "step", but a new way of thinking … always and from now on.
- ⚷ Healthy Thinking energizes you.
- ⚷ Healthy Thinking includes positive language and thinking habits
- ⚷ Eliminating PWs, "Problem Words", will greatly improve unhealthy thinking habits that are currently bringing you the things you do not want

Questions & Ideas

Note: Persons experiencing clinically diagnosed mood disorders or mental illness usually require varying degrees of assistance from professionals and support groups in strengthening their capacity for Healthy Thinking, wellness and recovery.

Chapter 3

DECIDE

Well, What Exactly _Do_ You Want?

Restless? Dissatisfied? Unhappy? It may seem difficult to believe, but most people would have difficulty quickly answering the question "What do you really want?" with respect to many aspects of their lives. Without knowing about, and using, the powerful strategy of "Deciding", many people flounder about, often having "OK lives", yet feeling vaguely dissatisfied. In the worst-case scenario, some people do not even attempt to identify what they want in order to be happy, and end up with miserable or troubled lives, and even addictions. Lacking the knowledge about how to apply the concept of Attraction to better their situation, many generations remain in a cycle of poverty, abuse and despair. The truth is … they are actually applying Attraction without knowing it, in a damaging or negatively repetitive way. _They are attracting what they are thinking about._

Think back to a time in your life when you knew exactly what you needed to do in order to change something, or obtain something you wanted. An example would be a time when you had an "Aha!" moment, and said to yourself, "Enough! I don't need this anymore!", and went on to change it. You made a clear, unwavering decision. That is what you need to get better at doing … all the time. What you in fact did, is _clarify_ what you _did not want_. You then Decided what _you did want_.

As a starting point on your way to being a "decider" instead of a "reed in the wind", get into the habit of asking yourself "What _do_ I want?" Whenever you are thinking discouraging or negative thoughts … Stop! Ask yourself "Hey! What is it that I _do_ want?" Re-direct your thinking on a regular basis.

The World's Most Powerful Question:

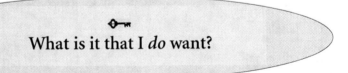

What is it that I _do_ want?

Step 1: DECIDE!

There are only <u>2</u> steps in the Attraction process. Everything you do in this new way of being fits into these two steps. Step # 1 is Decide.

Are you one of those people who ignore indicator lights on the panel of your vehicle? Now, what happens when we refuse to act on those annoying red lights and gauges? Indicator lights are part of your vehicle's warning system, designed to tell you "Hey! You need to make a decision *now*!" The natural law of Attraction has just such a warning system … your *feelings*.

Feelings Serve a Purpose

The fact that you are feeling vaguely, or greatly dissatisfied, is actually a good thing. That feeling is an "indicator". It indicates something is not quite right for you, for your life. The dissatisfaction you feel will help you Decide what it is that you *do* want. If you have a good idea of what it is that you want, but are not getting anywhere towards achieving it, the "Decide" step will catapult you forward. Deciding is the same as "asking" in the workings of Attraction. Decide, and you enable "it" to manifest. You will actually get the thing you are thinking about, and have Decided you want, if you follow the 2 Steps.

Note: With respect to certain desires, some of you may feel more at ease thinking of yourself as *asking*, while some of you may prefer the Deciding concept. It does not matter. Deciding or asking … Attraction's only job is to "notice" you have Decided you want that thing, and to get into action bringing it to you. Press on with whatever is comfortable for you.

Unpleasant feelings are "indicators" telling you that the thing you are thinking about is a thing you do *not* want. Your negative feelings are telling you to "Listen up! This is something you want less of, or none at all! Instead, you want XYZ!" Negative feelings are indicators that you should *Decide* about something here … there is always something that you want, or desire, that is different from what is triggering a negative feeling. Your emotions are there for a reason. We are continuously cued by our feelings, to move in a certain direction or another. We are continuously cued to act in a certain way or to do certain things, by the way these actions *feel* to us. Unfortunately, we are so overwhelmed by our daily lives and the expectations society has of us, that we are often tuned out and *away from* recognizing and acting correctly on our own feelings. Change this and watch what happens.

Making a Decision will generate a healthy feeling. It is an element of Healthy Thinking. Making a Decision to improve some aspect of your life that is truly unpleasant will generate a very good feeling, a very healthy feeling. It resembles the feeling of relief, even though at that moment, you think nothing has really changed. *Oh, but it has.* You have set Attraction and yourself in motion with the first important step. You have Decided.

Move Towards

In your Deciding thoughts, get into the habit of thinking of yourself as "moving towards" something, instead of "getting away from" what is happening now in your life. Thinking in this positive, deliberate manner is more powerful than the "getting away from" type of thought pattern.

Example:

Instead of Thinking or Saying:	Think or Say:
"I can't stand my apartment."	"I love the thought of moving to a new apartment
"I'll never get over her death."	"I know I will always remember her, and feel better with time."
"I'll never go shopping with him again!"	"From now on, I will go shopping with happy cheerful friends."
BA: "I'll never get the team to listen to my ideas."	BA: "There must be one person who is open to my type of ideas."
"I've got to get rid of this debt."	"I am moving towards a zero balance on my credit card."
"I'll never meet anyone in this town. I'll be single forever."	"I'm looking forward to meeting new people. You just never know when and where you will meet someone new."

You will know you are using Healthy Thinking and correct wording when it simply *feels* better. You feel hope, relief, or even excitement.

What Do I Decide to Attract First?

What a wonderful question to ask one's self! You may have so many things and situations in your life or your business that you want to change, that you currently feel overwhelmed. Take heart … it will all begin to improve, just as you intend it to. Attraction will help you.

A good idea would be to start with something from one of the areas I call, "The Big FOHR".

<u>They are:</u>

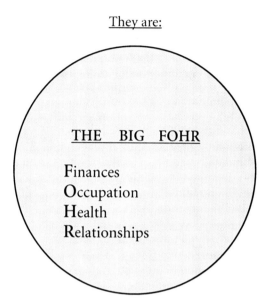

THE   BIG   FOHR

Finances
Occupation
Health
Relationships

First, from The Big FOHR, select *the* area in which you are having the most frustration and difficulty. For example, let us say you feel the most frustration and dissatisfaction with the state of your **F**inancial affairs.

Secondly, you now need to pinpoint the issues absolutely clearly, for yourself, by answering the following question. *What is the actual problem?* In other words, what is it that is bothering or upsetting you about your current situation? At first, you may answer that question with something like this:

"I don't have enough money."
"I'm in debt up to my ears."
"I want to buy a car, but I can't afford it."

Did you notice the key Problem Words in the above answers? It is useful to identify where you are using these negative PWs. In order to Decide what you want and to attract it, you will need to change your vocabulary. Remember: Your vocabulary is not just in your speech patterns, it is in your habitual thinking process. Your thinking process is like a "movie in your mind". From now on, you want *a happy ending to all your movies.* Start now. The more you eliminate PWs, or negative terminology, from your vocabulary and your mind, the more you will attract what you want instead of what you do not want.

What have you actually done, by identifying the PWs you are using when you think or talk about your Finances? You have begun to list the elements in your financial life ... the elements that you *do not want*. This is what is known in LOA as *contrast*. Being able to feel contrast, or what you *don't* want, is an important tool you have at your fingertips, to help you Decide what it is that you *do* want.

Note: If thinking about it makes you feel bad, it is something you *don't* want! That is contrast at work for you. That is the indicator light on the dashboard of your life. It is flashing red.

FEELINGS INDICATOR

Not sure what you really want?
Check your Feelings Indicator gauge.

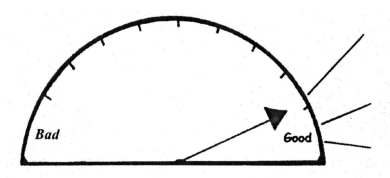

> Think about events,
> people, & things that make
> the needle on your Feelings
> Indicator gauge move over
> HERE ☼ ☺

Bad Feelings: Does thinking about something present in your life now make you feel *Bad?* Then this is something you want *less of,* or *none at all.* This "something" should be on your "What I Do <u>Not</u> Want" list. You need to Decide to attract a change to that "something". Perhaps you need to apply the law of Attraction to create a life free of that thing.

Good Feelings: Does thinking about something present in your life now, make you ***feel Good?*** Great! Acknowledge that good thing and keep thinking about how great it is to have this in you life. Does thinking about actually having a certain desire make you <u>*feel Good*</u>? Then you need to Decide to attract something that moves you in the direction of <u>*that*</u> change.

The following exercise will help you make your list of what it is you *do* want, with regards to The Big FOHR: Finances, Occupation, Health and Relationships.

Exercise # 4. Contrast/Decide

Example: Finances

Step 1. On an ordinary sheet of paper, start a list entitled "What I Do NOT Want":

    A. List all the Finance-related statements you commonly use with PWs in them.
    B. Add to this list all the things that cause you fear in your Financial affairs.
    C. Add the lack and the worries around money.
    D. Add the things you can't buy, do or enjoy now
    E. Keep going. Some people will list dozens, or even over 100 items

Note: For those of you who have a strong visual learning and communication style, you may want to find a beautiful piece of paper or stationary for the next part of this exercise.

Step 2. Turn the Un-Wanted into the Wanted

Now *on a new page*, take each item on your list, and *write down the opposite*. Write down what you *Do* want for each item you had on the first sheet of paper.
E.g., (On sheet 1) "I don't make enough money."
       (On sheet 2) "I want a 6-figure income."

Step 3. "Goodbye" to "What I Do NOT Want"

Now take the first page, the one with the unwanted items, fold it up and destroy it! Have fun destroying it. Play some fun music while you do this. You may want to burn it, shred it, chop it up as you enjoy a refreshing drink, or even crumple and tap dance on it until it is in shreds. It would also make great compost for the worms.

Feel free to re-write and revise the "What *Do* I Want" list, until you feel you have clearly outlined your Decision(s) … what you *do* want.

You now have a list of many things you want, in the Finances category. Now keep going for the other 3 of The Big FOHR: Occupation, Health, and Relationships.

How to Decide What to Attract First

Next, have some fun selecting what you want to attract first.

First, look at your "Finance-related" list. Spend some time checking off, circling or underlining the things that, *if* you had an unlimited supply of money and resources immediately, would be simple to "Get".

Note: These things may be simple to "get" because this group of desires is purely financial. However, some desires are linked to other desires. An example is "I want a whole new wardrobe in a size 10." Great! And … if you are a size 20 right now, it will take a little money plus a lifestyle change, plus some time to attract this. You *can* achieve that, of course, and everyone who has ever reached this weight loss goal has in fact done so by using … the natural law of Attraction, whether they realized it or not!

Let us say then, that you have 10 items (desires) that group nicely together in the Finance category. These would be items that require an infusion of money and/or other resources to obtain them. Examples would be:

- Zero balance on credit cards
- Bigger apartment
- Day care close to home
- New wardrobe for all members of the family
- Business loan to launch new venture

About Observing Contrast

What do you think the "Contrast/Decide" list started out like, concerning the items listed above? Think about that, *but do so only for a brief moment.* For example, for "Bigger Apartment", the original list item may have been "My apartment is so small I can't invite people over". That statement triggers negative feelings. Drop those feelings like a hot potato as quickly as possible! Never wallow in the negative feelings. You only want to identify problems briefly and somehow get to a *"better feeling"* place. Attraction will then get to work to bring you what you really want.

Never wallow in it. Observe contrast briefly. Always keep the time for focus on problems as short as you possibly can.

Secondly, on a scale of 1 to 10, score each item (desire) on your list, according to its importance to creating a better life for yourself. You may prefer to plot them on a continuum like the following:

---
1 2 3 4 5 6 7 8 9 1 0

Not Very Important   Very Important

Choose (circle, highlight or check) each item that scores 5 or more.

Congratulations! You have Decided on some important desires. And there will be many, as your life now wonderfully unfolds. By nature, we are destined to want more and different events, relationships, and things as we move through life. This is how we develop, grow and discover, as individuals and as societies.

One Big Wish

To this point, you have been "getting your head around" Deciding and clarifying what your desires are. We are wonderfully adept at wanting more and more things, happy events, and all manner of life improvements as our lives unfold. If you think your life was unfolding *before* you learned about Attraction … hang on to your horses! Now, the unfolding will be like nothing you have seen before … if that is what you desire. Or perhaps you will want a nice slow paced gradual improvement in your circumstances … it really is up to you.

Now it is time for you to attract a solution to your major area of concern. You will of course, by nature, be attracting all manner of improvements in other areas. However, it is important for you to focus on *something of significance*. Perhaps you have already reached all your main life goals, are happy, healthy, fulfilled, wealthy, partnered with the person(s) you most desire to be with, and are doing exactly what you want to do every day. Great! If not, you probably have one area you really need to improve on for you to simply *feel* better. Remember: law of Attraction gets into high gear *when you are having good feelings.*

Answer the following questions for yourself.

1.   What is that one area in your life that is "bringing you down" most?
2.   What is that one area where you seem to be forever repeating the same mistakes?
3.   What is that one area that causes you the most frustration, fear, anxiety or discouragement?
4.   In what area do you think that a significant improvement would make the most difference?

Your answer to each of the four questions above was probably the same.

Why is it important to attract significant improvements to the *one big issue* in your life? Because if you "fix up" ten "little issues", *the biggie* is still going to be there ... doing what? Making you feel bad! *Feeling Bad = Attracting Bad Stuff.* We want to attract good stuff.

<u>Now think back to "The Big FOHR":</u>

Finances
Occupation
Health
Relationships

From the above categories,

What is the "One Big Wish" that, if it came true for you, you would feel better about yourself?

What is the "One Big Wish" that, if it came true for you, you would feel more secure about life?

What is the "One Big Wish" that, if it came true for you, you would feel generally more relaxed?

What is the "One Big Wish" that, if it came true for you, you would feel just plain happier?

What is the "One Big Wish" that, if it came true for you, you would feel like you could tackle all the other issues?

That is what you need to focus on first. You will now apply the powerful forces of the natural law of Attraction to that "One Big Wish". And then of course, your other "life issues" and challenges will be improved along the way.

This does not mean you cannot think about other wonderful things you want to attract. On the contrary. You are changing your whole outlook on life, and in the process, all manner of improvements will occur. Apply Attraction to:

- having a pleasant drive every time you get into your car.
- your work day
- your business goals
- your day off
- your vacation
- your shopping
- your exercise program
- visiting the doctor
- your chat with your friend Larry on the phone

The list is wonderfully infinite.

Stating Your Decision

For now, as you read through the basics, simply hold on to your Decision statement. Call it *Decision One*. Keep it simple. For now, relax about wording, perfect statement form, or any other concerns you may have from pre-existing beliefs about "how you write or state these things for them to work". We will get to that shortly.

For the time being, simply use the following template, to clarify your Decision statement. Once you get *clarity* about your Decision, it will begin to manifest.

Decision One	
Example:	Your turn:
I have decided to move back to Arizona to live near my family.	I have decided to _____ _____ _____

Law of Attraction does not care what it is you have now Decided you want. In Deciding what you want, you have in fact "*asked*" or "*declared*". Attraction's only job is to bring it to you. In Deciding on your One Big Wish, you have "admitted to yourself" that this is what you really want. This is your main desire. You have accomplished Step 1 in the Attraction process. Now we will clarify, Energize and power up your desire in order to enable the natural law of Attraction to work on bringing it to you. Along the way, you will learn to apply the same 2-Step Attraction process to everything you want in life, from more Big Wishes, to parking spaces, to better relationships, to higher profit margins and endless other manifestations of abundance and joy.

Attract Abundance

Do you want to be more successful at attracting material desires?

⊶

Giving your attention to those material things
you will obtain, instead of the money required,
will cause abundance to flow
more easily.

Law of Attraction does not recognize those bits of paper, coins and bank transactions we call *money*. After all, if you received truckloads of money, but were marooned on a desert island and could not buy anything with it, you would not feel abundant at all, now would you? Rather, Attraction recognizes thoughts which are focused on the freedom, things and changes in your life you will gain as your wealth increases. You have more chance of winning cash draws when your focus is on *what* you will do or buy with that winning, instead of the cash prize.

Note: Problem gamblers can apply the law of Attraction to steer their focus *away from*, ticket buying, casinos and on-line poker, and *towards* a healthier lifestyle and the support required to cope with addiction. Attention, energy and focus can be given to a secure income from various sources, and a life of honest fulfilling relationships: Attraction will then respond with more of those positive manifestations.

Giving your attention to freedom, and the things you will obtain, instead of the money required to achieve these, will cause abundance to flow more easily.

For Example, instead of the money you need, focus on:

- ✓ The photos you will take with your new camera (it is easy to imagine photos)
- ✓ The huge donation you will make to your favourite charity (you can easily feel the joy of it coming true)
- ✓ Building a gym and pool facility for you and your employees to share (you can picture yourself and your team getting healthier and more productive)
- ✓ The new environmentally-friendly vehicle you will buy for you and every member of your family (you can feel the relief of making a difference to global warming)
- ✓ Leaving your current job and starting your own lucrative business (it is easy and pleasurable to think about all aspects of this major life change)
- ✓ The trip around the world you plan to take (you can dream of the places you will see and experience)

Did you notice the difference between how these examples feel, as opposed to simply trying to focus on the moment of cashing your first 5-figure pay-check, winning the lottery, or being handed an advance on a lucrative contract? It is much more natural and sustainable to access and maintain the good feelings required for your manifestations, when you can *focus on the end result, not the money*. This is what I call using the "Have-Want Gap" concept. In other words, you must create a gap between what you have now, and what you want … Attraction gets busy *filling the gap*.

Using The "Have—Want" Gap

Have < ....*GAP**............> <u>Want</u>

What you Have now:
- feels inadequate
- you want more
- you are tired of it
- you are bored with it
- you want something else instead
- thinking about it no longer makes you feel very good, or may even make you feel bad
- empty feeling

What you Want:
- Excites and motivates you
- Easy to daydream about
- Your thoughts return to it frequently
- Thinking about it makes you feel good
- Fulfillment

* Attraction gets busy filling this GAP (*bringing your desire to you*) when you <u>focus on What You Want</u>, not the money required.

If and when a particular desire is not materializing, it may be because you are not creating the positive feelings required within you when you think about the desire. You may be thinking about it until you are "blue in the face", but you need to ensure you have good, exciting, joyful feelings at the same time. These feelings are similar to those you felt the moment you Decided you would have that desire. Use the Exercises in this book and strengthen your ability to make it so. You will now learn how, by using Step 2 of the natural law of Attraction: Energize.

Proof Note: Sell Your Own Home … Times 3 !

Property #1: In the late eighties, I had purchased a "fixer-upper" in a beautiful neighborhood. My daughters and I enjoyed living there, yet I had decided to complete the renovations, and sell the home for a profit, in order to buy a larger, newer home in the same neighborhood. Against the dire warnings of real estate agents, I decided to sell it privately. I prepared my home for viewing, and advertised in the local paper, with the date of my open house. I gave this project a lot of positive attention, energy and focus, and kept my thoughts optimistic. One agent who was aiming to list the property for me, warned that I would have trouble selling it because of its age, and that I would be lucky to get $119,000 for it. I needed to sell it for $125,000 to meet my financial plan for the next purchase. I sold it on the day of my first and only open house. The buyer literally stepped into the foyer, and said, "I'm buying your house. Please don't show it to any one else!" By the end of the day, I had two offers, and sold it for my asking price, $125,000.

Property #2: Years later, it was time to move on, as I had met my future husband, and wedding bells were ringing. With one daughter out of the nest, and the other finishing university, I was ready to sell again. I made the decision, put my energy attention and focus on the sale. This time, we were in a buyer's market, and I needed all the help I could get. I followed the same process, advertising on my own, visualizing it sold, making notes about the end result I wanted, and soon had an appointment to show the property. Disappointed that the couple did not show up, I was surprised by a knock at the door. Another couple happened to drive by at the time of the no-show appointment, knocked on the door, and asked if they could see the house immediately. I invited them in, and as soon as they stepped into the entrance, the woman declared, "It's perfect! We're buying it. Please don't show it to anyone else." And it was sold.

<u>Property #3:</u> My husband John and I purchased our first home together, a quaint country cottage in a rural area. We renovated and upgraded it, with the intent to sell it and purchase a larger home in the city, close to our families and our lakeside cottage. We had a fixed amount we intended to get for it. We wrote this figure down, with a statement like "88 River Drive—Sold! For $150,000!" We talked about how easy it would be to sell it, though rural properties in our area typically took about one year to sell. We had a web site prepared, which I had spent a lot of time working on—a great visualizing/Energizing strategy. We had not even advertised it or uploaded the web site yet, when John's Mother called us because she heard a friend of a friend of friend's son might be interested. John called the young couple, who turned out to be perfect for this property. They quickly came over, and fell in love with the home. The deal was closed in 3 days, for the asking price.

Recap Chapter 3: DECIDE

- Think and talk about what you *do* want
- Feelings: Negative ones are indicators that show you are thinking about something you *don't* want
- Feelings: Positive ones are indicators that show you are thinking about something you <u>do</u> want
- The Big FOHR: Finances Occupation Health Relationships
- One Big Wish: The Solution to your major area of concern. If you could make this One Big Wish materialize, everything else would improve
- Decide what you *do* want using the Contrast/Decide exercise. Give that your attention, energy and focus.
- Focus on the end result of increased abundance, not the money

Questions & Ideas

Chapter 4

ENERGIZE

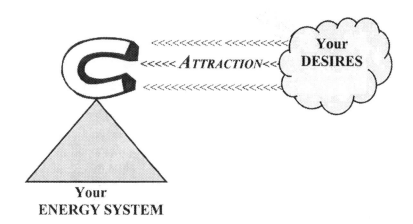

Energy

Energy is the *stuff* of the universe. It is what everything is made of. It is what *we* are made of. It is what our thoughts are made of. This fact of nature is perfect. It is in perfect harmony with the natural law of Attraction. It is perfect because when we can control energy … we can create, enabling us to invent and build things, or even … make things happen. Our thoughts are the *only* things we can control. Even persons living with paralysis or other immobilizing conditions use their "thought lives" to create joy for themselves. *You* have a thought life. We can line up the energy of our thoughts and transform our lives into more abundant, joyful experiences. We can enjoy spectacular, safe, satisfying healthy lives. That is our destiny. That is your destiny.

Good Feelings Bring Good Things

This chapter is all about helping you learn to *stay focused on your desires, while accessing good feelings.* This is what is meant by Energizing, "Step 2" in the Attraction process. Learning to use this simple, yet little-known process will help you manifest your desires at a rate and speed you previously thought impossible. The exercises are simple. You will find them very enjoyable, and may even find yourself having some fun, all by yourself!

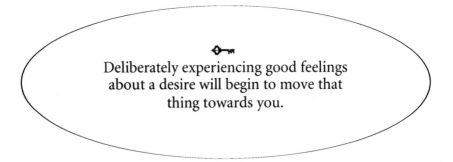

Deliberately experiencing good feelings
about a desire will begin to move that
thing towards you.

Step 2: ENERGIZE

There are really only *2 steps* in the Attraction process. Now you will learn the basics of Energizing your desires so that the law of Attraction can begin moving those desires towards you. If you are like many people, you must improve your way of thinking, to apply positive energy, attention and focus to what it is that you *do want*. You will now learn the Healthy Thinking strategies which will Energize you and allow the manifestation of your desire.

Negative People Suck The Life Right Out of You.

Have you ever been feeling particularly good and then found yourself engaged in a conversation with a person who was in a negative mood? What did that feel like? Did you want to go home and exercise, or jog in the fresh air? Did you want to tackle the 100's of unread emails in your In Box? Did you want to finally open up the "I Want a Raise" discussion with your boss? Did you suddenly feel like starting to work on your company's Strategic Plan? Probably not. Chances are you felt deflated, and a little bit more tired than when the conversation began.

Protect Yourself: Get and Stay Positive

Protect yourself. The next time the negative person shows up in your life, you will be armed and ready. *You will politely and relentlessly respond in a positive way.* Two things can happen. The negative person may just go away to seek a more "like-minded individual". Or, they may be stopped in their tracks, respond in a neutral or even pleasant manner, and go away wondering, "What just happened?"

You have time for positive interactions only! You are on a mission to change something in your life, perhaps your whole life experience. You are on a mission to attract only the things and people you *want* into your personal or business life. It is possible that eventually, this person will avoid you all together. If this person is a loved one, you could apply the Attraction process to deliberately create a more positive relationship. The dynamics between you could change in a positive way. Remember how the law of Attraction works? If you keep allowing yourself to have negative feelings each time you interact with a person, law of Attraction will simply continue to bring you more of the same experiences.

Note: For those of you in painful, damaging relationships, the law of Attraction will work for you as well. You will eventually find yourself in an improved life situation, if you stick with it. The first thing you must do, should you be in such a situation is to use the strategies in this book to attract healthy, positive, helpful people. The decisions you will need to make will become clearer, easier, exciting, and you will become Energized to change your life. You deserve it.

PW Reminder

PWs: Remember to focus on eliminating Problem Words and phrases from your vocabulary and your thoughts. (See Chapter 2)

> The problem with all negative thought or spoken words is that *LOA does not differentiate between negative or positive, it simply brings you what you think about.* Stay focused on what you *want.*

Example:

Dan *Part 1.*

Dan says, "I hate having to drive through all this construction every darn day!"

Guess what, Dan? You will end up driving through lots of construction sites, roadwork and bridges under repair ... because you are attracting them!

Attraction only picks up Dan's vibes of "drive through construction sites". Dan gave "driving through construction" energy, attention and focus. And so ... law of Attraction *brings more of that to Dan.* Attraction works especially hard at bringing it to Dan in this case because he gave the thought a shot of emotion. He said, "I *hate* ..." This is a powerfully charged Problem Word ... a nasty PW, supercharged to bring you more what? More stuff you do *not* want!

Dan *Part 2*

Dan, having just learned how to apply Attraction, will now choose to say, and think something like this:

"I love it when I get to drive all the way to work and the roads are clear, the traffic is moving smoothly, and I hit every green light!."

Guess what Attraction will bring to Dan now?

Master Your Thoughts

Be a master corrector of your own limiting negative thoughts … until positive thoughts become second nature.

In order to "get good" at focusing on positive thoughts, as well as the things, people and events you want more or, instead of the things that are bothering you about your life, you need to repeatedly correct yourself. Our education system, our governmental organizations, the media and much of how our society is set up, are laced with anxiety-producing elements, fear mongering, and processes or experiences that produce anxiety within us. You must re-focus on the positive at every possible opportunity in order to re-train your mind to attract good things to you. Replacing negative vocabulary and thoughts with positive ones is key to helping you correct any negative thoughts, key to Healthy Thinking.

You will begin to see an increase in the speed and frequency of Attraction bringing you more of what you truly want, as you gain control over your negative thoughts. The sooner you become what is now known as *"someone with a positive attitude"*, the sooner your life will improve.

It is a well-known fact that:

✓   Positive people are healthier and live longer.

✓   Positive people get the jobs.

✓   Positive people have more friends.

✓   Positive people get married.

✓   Positive people attract more of what they want into their lives.

✓   Positive people weather adversity, survive disasters and thrive where others fail

Energy System

Build your own unique system to Energize your Attraction process … your Energy System. Your Energy System will "cue" you to *think* about your goals, wants and desires as often as possible. Thinking about what you *do* want more often will increase the number and speed of "good stuff" coming your way, including people, things and events. This is what is meant by *giving attention, energy and focus.*

What is an Energy System?

The natural law of Attraction's only "job" is to deliver to you what you think about: your *Desires*. Your *thoughts are the magnets* powerfully pulling things, people and events to you, *continuously*. The *force* between your thoughts and the desires you have *is Attraction*. And the force is *already* with you!

An Energy System is anything that works for *you* to help you stay focused, giving your attention to, and thinking about the things you Decided you want to attract. Everyone's Energy System is unique. Yours will help you find and maintain *good feelings*, key to Attracting what you want. Strangely, without this Energy System, all of us can easily "forget" to put our attention, energy and focus on what it is that we *do* want, effectively sabotaging *ourselves*! Life is hectic. Life is busy. There are many things to do, many distractions. You need a simple system to stay focused.

YOUR UNIQUE ENERGY SYSTEM

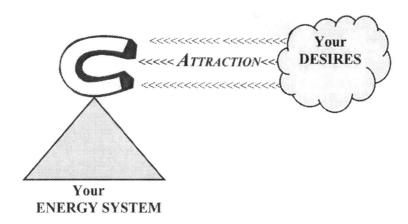

How to Visually Energize Your Desires

Most people are "visual operators" to a large extent. We think in pictures. We enjoy observing, and appreciate the aesthetic qualities of things around us. We learn more easily when pictures are shown, or when we can "see" the end result. A popular Energy System element promoted by teachers of Attraction and goal setting experts, is that of posting pictures of the things you want, in and around you at home or at work. Simply observing visual cues about what you want will in fact subconsciously register that thing in your mind. By placing the pictures where you see them frequently, you will also be prompted to think about, daydream, and Energize your desire. LOA will "notice" that thought or thing in your mind, and get to work delivering it to you.

Note: Successful companies use visual cues in their offices and factories, effectively keeping everyone focused on the same desires and overall goals. Professional athletes, astronauts and cancer patients are all taught to visualize the desired result, in order to maximize their chances of success.

BA: Organizational as well as governmental public relations ads and materials depict scenes where things are running smoothly, with the client being well-taken care of by the service provided. They are depicting the desired result or the interaction.

Rather than visualizing, or trying to see things in their mind, some people find other methods easier. These people become frustrated trying to "visualize". *That's OK!* Whatever works best for you, to help cue you back to thinking about and *feeling good* about your desire is great! Even people with low vision and blindness visualize and *see* things in their own minds, in their own way. Ideally, however, learning to visualize is a strategy you should learn and apply as much as possible. It will serve you well.

Note: If you find yourself frustrated by trying to visualize, or seeing a picture in your mind, try the following. Instead of a picture, simply imagine a color you like, or a large colored screen, on which your desire is *written* or typed and scrolling up or across, like a computer screen saver. Visualizing, like any other exercise, gets easier the more you practice it.

<u>BA</u> <u>Example</u>: Imagine your One Big Wish is to open a second branch of your company in the Bahamas. Instead of trying to visualize the new office in the Caribbean, you could imagine a royal blue screen on which is continually scrolling "Lisa and Rick Blank hold successful launch of XYZ Advertising, in the Caribbean sun!" You could even imagine it looking like a newspaper headline.

Visual Energizers

Choose from any or all of the following. Build them into your unique Energy System to Energize your desire. You may surprise yourself and become a lot more "visual" than you ever were. Visual cueing in one form or another, is a powerful business and organizational tool, and is used in every organization and successful commercial enterprise.

The Dream Board

Obtain a piece of bristle board or cardboard. Start collecting photos, or magazine and catalogue pictures, of things, people and events you have Decided you want to attract. Stick them on. Make a collage. There is no need to be artistic here. Have some fun. Cast aside any awkwardness you may have about doing this. Relax about what your family and friends may think. This is the time to get serious about changing *your* life. Your family may even begin to ask questions and become your LOA colleagues! Children love this type of thing. Encourage them to post pictures and collages as well. Partners, husbands and wives will get curious sooner or later. You may find the opportune time to share with them your new life-changing ideas, by simply answering their questions. Should they choose to learn about and deliberately apply Attraction, as you are now doing, *together ... you will be unstoppable.*

Make your poster or collage as creatively unique as you wish. Actually spending time making the poster is a perfect example of an Energizing activity. The whole time you are doing it, and adding to it day by day, you are giving your desire(s) attention, energy and focus.

 ## Carry-On Cues

Put photos and pictures of your desires in your wallet, in your bag, suitcase, briefcase, your pockets, any place you may need to access when you are away from home. You will then surprise yourself with cues to bring you back to thinking about what you *do* want.

 ## Workplace Reminders

Most people like to be a little more subtle in the workplace. This is unless, of course, you are fortunate enough to be in a workplace now, where positive thinking, goal setting and success strategies like the law of Attraction are the way you do business. At work, you may want to use "Code Cues". Code cues are acronyms you create as reminders for yourself. You can use sticky notes on your computer frame, or jot notes in your day timer.

Examples of Code Cues:
BNC = Brand New Car
NH + New Home
SM = Soul Mate
ER = Early Retirement
SI = Sales Increasing
AD = Absenteeism Decreasing

 Clothing & Jewelry

Chose to wear a colour or a type of jewelry that for you, signifies a certain desire. For example, for you, a rich dark green may signify the Attraction of a new career with double the salary. Wearing gold coloured jewelry or buttons, or even a type of tie, may cue you to think about the soul mate you are in the process of attracting. You simply choose what clothing or jewelry to link up with a particular desire. Clothing and jewelry are also tactile, or "touch" cues for your Energy System.

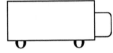 **Car Cues**

Include at least one picture or object in your vehicle, which reminds you and makes you think about the desire you most want to attract. You can tape the picture to your console, your steering wheel, or any spot you will "for sure" be glancing at, at least once during each drive.

Note: Attract this. Each time you get into a vehicle, think the following, "*I intend to have a safe and pleasant journey with a relaxed and timely arrival at my destination.*"

Computer Cues

Use backgrounds, cursors, screen savers and any other visual software that reminds you of your desires. When possible, take a 10 to 30-second "eyes closed and resting" break, to re-focus on positive thoughts. During those moments, you can also roll your shoulders and do neck stretches, both healthy exercises, which will give you a pleasant feeling at the same time.

Scrap Book

Scrap booking has become a multi-million dollar industry. Why? Because people enjoy looking at the things they love, the things they want, and the things that bring them good memories and good feelings. Beautiful scrapbooks can be purchased for less than the cost of a movie, or you can make one out of a simple scribbler or notebook. Simply start collecting the pictures that match the things, people and events you want to attract, and start pasting! You can flip through it while you are eating breakfast, or during commercials, or as a regular Energizing exercise to picture your improved life or business.

You now have several parts, or components, to include in your own unique, personally designed and engineered Energy System. The idea is to do *whatever works for you* to Energize your desires and enable their manifestation. Choose one element, or as many as you wish. Invent your own, and have some fun building your Energy System.

Proof Note: Winning The Computer

Before it was common for families to own home computers, I knew that a computer would be of great value for my growing girls' education, not to mention for my class preparation work. I was writing a textbook at the time, by hand, with the rough drafts going to a paid typist-editor. However, I could not afford to buy a personal computer, even if I did know how to type.

The college I worked for was raffling off used computers at the main campus across the city. A full system computer and four other lesser models were to be raffled. I was determined to win one, and not just any one, but the big one … the one with the printer. Intent on winning, I cut out a picture of a personal computer and photo copied it many times. I stuck this little picture everywhere in our house, including on the fridge. Next I talked to my daughters all about how great it would be to win it, and I told them to *imagine us winning it*. I also added the words "Win Me" to the pictures.

On the day of the draw, my dozen or so overworked colleagues and I had procrastinated and not yet deposited our tickets in at the other campus across the city! I collected the tickets from each of my coworkers, drove across town just in time for the big event, and found my way to the contest room. Many witnesses were there and because I had a stack of them, every ticket was veri-fied by the contest organizer before it was dropped into the drum. As I was chatting with a friend, the draw took place, and sure enough, I was the winner of The Big One! I took the computer and printer home that day. In no time, I was learning to type, and completed my first book, a nursing study textbook. Holly and Sarah were soon little home computer wizards, and Holly actually ended up doing a lot of typing for me over the years.

Right now, there are pictures of all sorts, here and there in my home office and elsewhere in our home. My husband and I have placed pictures of our common goals and desires on our bedroom dresser mirror, on the fridge and in the bathroom. Thanks to our Energy Systems and the law of Attraction, it is always only a matter of time before our latest dreams (or something better) materialize, in our business and personal lives.

How to Energize Your Desires with Sound

For most of us, and for some more than others, the auditory mode is another powerful learning style we use. Sound can Energize your desires and is a very effective component of anyone's Energy System.

Try these techniques.

Self Talk

Consciously or not, we all talk to ourselves "in our heads". Talking to our-selves aloud, verbalizing, or "affirming", is an effective way to Energize our desires as well. You may feel a bit odd talking to yourself at first, but at times, you may find it quite useful in "getting the feeling" you need to get, to give your desire energy, attention and focus. Remember ... anything that Energizes your desire keeps your Energy System well fueled.

Say The Words

Who is the CEO of your life? You are. Successful leaders are fearless in saying what needs to be said in order to "get the job done". Sports teams use this strategy when practicing their pre-game cheers and chants. These "Rah! Rah! We Can Do It!" cheers and jingles are highly effective.

Successful leaders *say the words* that others hesitate to say.

BA: We as individuals in charge of our own lives, as well as leaders in charge of organizations, can increase our successes in achieving goals of all types by getting better at "Saying The Words". Energize your desires with sound: act and speak *as if* you or your team is *already* successful in achieving the goal.

Practice the following Exercise in order to increase your skill at saying the words that bring success.

Exercise # 5. Say The Words

Step 1: Think
Sit comfortably, near a mirror. Close your eyes and visualize or simply think of your desire quietly. Think of a phrase or statement you will next speak out loud, in order to Energize your desire.

Step 2: Say The Words
Now open your eyes, stand up and just "Say The Words"! Say it loud, with Energy, and with feeling. Smile. Put an excited look on your face. Say it 3 times.

Example: Desire—Succeeding in a job interview and being offered the position
1. Sit comfortably, near a mirror. Close your eyes and for 30 seconds, picture yourself doing fabulously well in the interview for your new job. Think of phrases like "Wow! I was great in that interview!"

2. Now open your eyes, stand up and say 'Wow! I was great in that interview! I aced it! They loved me!" Say it loud, with energy, and with feeling. Smile. Put an excited look on your face. Say it 3 times while looking at yourself in the mirror.
Note: bursting out laughing at yourself can occur as a great side effect of this exercise ☺

"What if I Don't Believe Myself When I Say or Think It?"

Desire statements or affirmations that are very different from your current reality may be difficult for your mind to accept at first. You will get better at it and eventually master the "affirming" of desires you once thought impossible. What does work, even for the beginner, is *to create and use affirmations that are true for you.*

For example, imagine you want to lose 100 lbs. If you say to yourself, "I am slim, firm and fit." Well, you may have difficulty with that statement at first because the opposite is currently true. What is true, however, is that if you have truly *Decided* to lose 100 lbs, you have in fact already begun the *process* of losing the pounds, by making the firm Decision to do so.

What you may want to state initially is something like this:

- "I am in the process of losing 100 pounds."
- "It feels wonderful to imagine myself in a new bathing suit."
- "I love thinking about what my old friends will say when they see me and my new fit body."
- "I am excited about walking farther and farther every day now, and joining the exercise class as soon as I have lost the first 50 pounds."

Do you see the difference? More importantly, do you *feel* the difference? All these statements are true. With these types of statements, or what we will now call '*A Statements*', you will be comfortable and *feel good* as you think about new possibilities. The good feelings that accompany your statements are Energizers and will be part of your Energy System.

Auditory Inspiration

There are many great teachers of the natural law of Attraction, and of the concepts associated with it. Audio strategies are often promoted in their teachings. Attraction is a natural scientific universal law at work, and will eventually be accepted as such, just as Gravity has been. Attraction is the real story behind all effective self-improvement and success "methods". Until your own thinking process is corrected in order to allow your desires to show up in your life more often, you will find cues of all types helpful. Cues will "bring you back" to thinking about your desire. For those of us who have a strong auditory learning style, or love of sound and music, cues of that nature will help greatly.

Simple sound cues in your Energy System can remind you of your desire, and help you simultaneously experience good feelings. The moment of your desire's appearance in your life will then occur sooner.

Examples:

- Decide that every time your telephone rings, your desire will pop into your mind.
- Associate a popular uplifting song with your desire, and visualize "as if it is already here", through the entire song.
- Link the sound of horns blowing in traffic to thoughts of your desire
- Make your alarm clock your friend. Re-program your feelings about your alarm clock. When it goes off, every morning, kick LOA into high gear by making that sound a cue to start your day by thinking about your fondest wish.

The following Auditory Energizer exercise is an effective tool you will enjoy. You will need a clock or a watch, or perhaps a kitchen timer, and a recording device. A good old-fashioned tape recorder, or any electronic recording device will work. Tiny new recording/dictating devices are now available at any electronics or computer store. These fit in the palm of your hand, are simple to operate, and inexpensive.

Note: This is a powerful exercise which helped me find and attract my wonderful husband. Read about our story in the next Proof Notes box.

Exercise # 6. Auditory Energizer

Step 1. Write It Down
Write down 6 to 10 "A" Statements (positive statements or affirmations) about your desire. (More detail about the correct method for statement wording is explained in Chapter 6. There is no need to use perfect A Statement form yet.)

Step 2: Record
Chose your favorite CD of relaxing or uplifting music. It must be music that plays continuously for at least 15 minutes. Play the CD quietly in the background.
Start recording with 1 minute of just the music playing.

Now continue recording, with you speaking your Statements out loud 3 times each, slowly and with feeling. Feel and imagine as if "your desire is already here" as you speak.

Pause between each set of 3 Statements while you take 1 or 2 quiet relaxing breaths.

End the recording with a "Thank You" type of closing statement or acknowledgment of your choosing, followed by 1 minute of just the music playing.

Step 3: Over and Over and Over ...

Now listen to your tape or CD every day at least once, ideally in an area where you can be alone and quiet. Just before sleeping, is an excellent time. If you find that the Auditory Energizer Exercise "Energizes" you too much, enjoy it in the daytime. Put it on your IPod™ or Walkman™ and enjoy it during walks. You can even let it play in your car as you are driving.

Proof Note: Attracting True Love

<u>The Strategy:</u> I had been single for 13 years, raising my daughters while climbing the health care career ladder. I was rather enjoying the dating scene, yet yearned to settle down with my ideal life partner. Having had a few serious boyfriends, made some less-than-ideal choices, and having "kissed enough frogs", I Decided it was time to find the right man for me, and enjoy a happy married life.

Having experimented with positive thinking and goal-setting strategies for some time, I was in fact using the law of Attraction without realizing it. I did use what I knew then as "affirmations", for various things in my life, with varying degrees of success. Seeking a way to find my future husband, I Decided to make a cassette recording using positive statements about what I wanted. I used Baroque music for the background, and with headphones on, I relaxed in my room, usually lying down, and listened to it every day at least once. I included a visual scene in my thoughts, where my future husband was on a road, walking towards me.

My affirmations included ones about how he would "be" with me, how he would respect and cherish me, be faithful and fun to be with, healthy, and how he would enjoy and care about my family. I wanted someone I could "be myself" barefaced, in sickness and in health. I do not remember the affirmations I used.

Note: In my home, I hung artwork that depicted happy couples and men cherishing women in a loving, adoring and respectful way. Knowing the value of putting the right kinds of images in one's field of everyday vision, I had deliberately chosen these prints.

<u>Manifestation:</u> I had been planning to attend an annual lakeside party at a friend's beautiful summer home in Sheguindah, on Manitoulin Island. A girlfriend who was supposed to come with me backed out and I had no intention of going alone. My friend the host however, insisted I come and talked me into going. No sooner was I settled on the deck, feeling a little out of place, when a small plane piloted by another friend of mine, landed at dockside.

Out stepped John, soon to be the love of my life, guitar in hand. Having been genetically blessed with a good singing voice, I have been singing since my mother taught me to sing the Tennessee Waltz © at the age of five. I did not however, play any instrument at the time, and thought, "Well, at least there is someone here I can sing with." But then ... the moment I met John, there was a powerful Attraction. The chemistry was there. I soon learned he had all the qualities I had been thinking and asking about in my recorded tape. We were married at a beautiful resort in Jamaica 2 ½ years later and are now living happily ever after.

The Other Senses Are Energizers Too

Your senses of smell, taste and touch are effective triggers to Energize you as well. They are part of the Energy System already operating within you. *The idea is always to cue you to think about your desire(s) while having a good feeling at the same time.* Here are some ideas to help you put all your senses to work to attract more of what you want into your life.

The Bath

Make a Decision to think about things you truly want, every day at bath or shower time. Pick two components of your regular routine. These could be the use of a particular soap you love the smell of, the taste of your favourite toothpaste, or the feel of the plush floor mat. Whether in the shower or tub, always spend 10-30 seconds minimum with your eyes closed, thinking clearly about your dreams. Begin today, associating these sensations to thinking about your desires. Every time you go through your daily bath or shower ritual, at least two of your senses will then cue you to focus on your desires. Just as a certain scent may remind you of your loved one, your magnificent servant brain will soon "automate" this process, and you will not have to consciously make the Decision to think about things you want. Attraction will ensure your brain kicks in to action, and your desire will appear on the movie screen in your mind.

Why Do I Need All These Cues?!?

You are only human. Even masters of Attraction can and do attract stuff we do not want, and even "forget" about our desires easily, due to the onslaught of information coming at us, and everyday distractions we encounter, not to mention our busy work and family lives. We use cues and our unique Energy Systems to re-focus on what we *do* want.

The beauty of Attraction is that once you have re-trained your thinking process to be a more focused one, you will not *need to* continuously use the cues unless you *want to.* Most people however, do get positive feelings from the use of cues, find these triggers useful, and therefore speed up Attraction by deliberately using them.

Regardless of whether we are conscious of it or not, we are actually attracting exactly what we are thinking about already. In one form or another, the thoughts we think about are always eventually materializing in our lives, sometimes exactly as they played out in the movie screen of our mind. If you are still doubtful, go back to your Co-incidences Exercise (Chapter 1) and review your notes.

The sooner we Decide to learn and to apply the law of Attraction deliberately, the sooner we will have more of what we truly want to be, have and do in our lives.

This is why it is critical to use whatever cues we need in the beginning, to get our wonderful servant brain to work, not against us, but *for* us.

Your Servant Brain

Science is just scratching the surface in learning about the incredible power of the human brain. Through this important research, discoveries about how the brain functions are occurring daily. Psychologists, psychiatrists and scientists are thinking constantly about questions relating to the brain, and they are formulating hypotheses. Hypotheses are theories. "We're not sure ... but maybe ... well, let's do an experiment ..." is how the conversation often flows for researchers in the "mind" lab.

One of the most delightful discoveries about the brain is that *thoughts are things*. Thoughts produce waves! These waves can be measured. (*For us Science and Nature fans—doesn't this stuff get you excited?!?*)

We have also known, for thousands of years, that the law of Attraction exists as a natural universal energy force. Some have known that by consciously applying LOA, by thinking about what we want, that which we thought about appeared. The brain, via its *thinking process*, is therefore our servant. Your brain, or the mind within it, can focus or give attention to particular things, and in doing so, enlists the law of Attraction to get to work for us. With your mind and Attraction working together, the results are inevitable: *manifestation.*

I Feel Good!!!

James Brown ... Thank You! We have all heard that classic R & B song "I Got You"©, with the "world's most energizing" lyric:

> *I Feel Good!!!' ... na na na. Na na na.*
> *I knew that I would now!*

> ♪ ♪ ♪ ♪ ♪ ♪ ♪ ♪ ♪ ♪ ♪

After a workshop to learn how to deal with stress in the workplace, some of my colleagues installed the sound bite from the late, great James' Brown, above, on their computer desktop. They listen to it occasionally during their workday as a quick cure for stress ... a *feel good* cue.

This little combination of musical notes is a perfect example of a trigger that is guaranteed to get you *feeling good!* James Brown reached the pinnacle of stardom and his music will go down in history. Of course, he did this, not because he was a "chosen one", or went to a conservatory, or had parents who could afford to give him voice or guitar and music writing lessons. He achieved this by thinking it and Attracting what he wanted.

Note: James Brown passed on to that R&B band on the other side on December 25th 2006.

What does music have to do with Attracting *What I Want*? Everything.

> You will speed up the process of Attraction in direct proportion to the amount of good feelings you have, as you repeatedly think about your desires.

Read the above statement over, and over again. It is the essence of Step 2, "Energize".

Use uplifting music to Energize you at any time, and help you experience the feelings that powerfully move you towards what you want out of life. For some it is Hip Hop or Pop, for others it may be Classical or Gospel, Rock or Jazz.

Whatever works for you or your organization is what should be part of your Energy System.

What *Is* a Feeling and Why is it Important to LOA?

I have been in the professional health care field for over 30 years. I have been at the bedside of many dying cancer patients, and in the meeting and boardrooms of many health care organizations. There is one thing that is true 100% of the time. *Feelings count greatly, in the chance for success regarding the goal, whatever that may be.* Here are some vivid examples.

Pain and Suffering †

This anecdote took place in the late 70's, well before today's pain control treatments were in use.

A young, very reserved woman, in the latter stages of metastatic cancer (cancer that has spread), wakes after another long and restless night, is lying in her hospital bed, the pain returning for another day. Again this morning, large amounts of purulent odorous drainage are coming out of the dressing on what is left of her cancer-ridden breast. Her husband is coming in shortly and the complex dressing is scheduled to be changed this afternoon. The nurse assesses the situation and though the patient claims to be "fine", senses the true state she is in. She offers, "Would you like me to change your dressing now instead of giving you your bath?" "Oh please, would you?" the patient says, "then my husband won't have to see me like this. He's coming in early." She is very happy, begins to *feel good*, and the pain goes away. The woman had been lying there, hoping and wishing somehow, her husband would not see her like this, and smell the awful dressing. In her mind, she visualizes herself fresh and neat, ready to receive her husband's visit. The nurse has been professionally trained in assessment, including the skills of evaluating the patient's *feelings*. She can then provide the type of excellent care required. The patient's goals (desires) can then be attained.

Music Creates Feelings ♫

We have all experienced the power of music in our lives, countless times. Examples:

- ⚿ You are at a funeral, though you were not particularly close to the deceased. An angel-voiced singer, accompanied by a highly skilled organist, begins to sing Ave Maria. Your throat tightens up, the tears begin to flow, and you are one with the family in experiencing the feeling or vibration of grief

⚷ You are watching a horror movie. Until now, there has been no accompanying musical score, only sound effects and dialogue. But then … the eerie music we all associate with fear begins. Weird high-pitched screeches, gloom and doom organ and bass drums … haunting violins … and your "I'm about to get scared out of my wits" radar goes off the map.

⚷ You are at a wedding. The day has been a long one, you ate a bit too much delicious food, and you would really like a nap. However, the band starts up and blasts into a rocking rendition of "Mustang Sally"©. Suddenly, you and most of the crowd are up dancing your toes off, feeling happy and energized.

By learning to use music as a cue, or trigger, to accessing good feelings when thinking about your desires, you will have increased the power of your Energy System.

BA: Companies use this strategy in their choice of jingles to sell you their products. Their desire is for you to buy that product. Advertising professionals chose jingles by the jingle's ability to trigger a good feeling about the product in the listener—you … the eventual purchaser of the product.

You can sell yourself on your own desires and put this tried and true technique to work for you.

The following is an exercise based on a musical game we have all played at one time or another.

Exercise # 7. Sing It ♫ ♪

Step 1: Pick a tune
Decide on a simple song you really like, that makes you feel good ...
energized. Hum or sing a bit of it to be sure. Christmas carols or
childhood songs are easy to use for this exercise.

Step 2: Create lyrics to Energize your desire
On a piece of paper, create some new lyrics to this song, lyrics to match
your desire.

Step 3: Sing! That's right ... it is just you, your Energy System and the
law of Attraction. No one is listening. Talent is not required. Just sing it.
You can sing it in your car, in the shower, anywhere you feel
comfortable.

Example: Jill has decided to Attract more joy into her life. To the tune of
"Happy Birthday", she came up with this:

> I'm attracting more joy.
> I'm attracting more joy.
> More joy is coming to me.
> I'm attracting more joy.

Jill is frequently heard softly humming this little tune. *But more than just
a little tune,* her own unique lyrics are a powerful force Attracting more
joy to Jill.

If you find yourself laughing aloud at the silliness of it all, great! That's a good
thing, since that laughter and moment of fun is a great feeling to "link up" to
your visualization about your desire. Remember, feeling good vibrations when
thinking about what you want will bring it to you. This is Energizing. This is a
great working component of your unique Energy System.

Vibrations

Remember "thoughts are things" or "Quantum physics" from earlier? Your feelings are actually powerful thoughts, or vibrations, that are measurable, using scientific imaging equipment. If you could see them, they might look something like this, emanating from you:

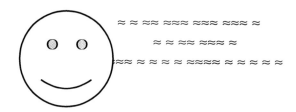

The actual microscopic appearance may be more of a straight line. For our purposes, it really does not matter. What matters is that *your feelings are actually vibrations you are emitting, or "giving off"*. Thoughts are vibrations of energy. Everything is energy. That is what Einstein was trying to tell us with this equation:

$$E = MC^2$$

(Energy = Mass x Speed of Light in a Vacuum)

Vibrations are all around us. They are in us. They affect everything we do. They *are* everything we do. Much of the material written about the natural law of Attraction includes the term "vibrations" either instead of, or interchangeably with the word "feelings". These terms *are* interchangeable in fact, when applied to Attraction. Whenever you see the term "feelings" in this book, you can think of it as the term "vibrations", if you prefer, and vice versa. For our purposes, they are the same thing.

Note: Some will argue that there is no such thing as a "vibration" emanating from us or from our thoughts in any way. They are misguided. Many scientific studies and biofeedback systems have absolutely proven, and provided the scientific evidence that, we do in fact give off vibrations, continuously. Studies show irrefutably that the vibrations we emit from our brain activity changes as we think different thoughts.

How Does This Help Me Attract What I Want?

Ever since humankind began discovering the laws of nature, we looked for ways to use these wonderful facts of life in order to invent and create new things, as well as to simplify and improve our lives. The following is a list of some of nature's laws which have been harnessed to help us achieve our desired purposes:

Law	Example of How we Use It
Gravity (Newton)	Intravenous Drip
Buoyancy (Archimedes)	Boat lifts in canals
$E = MC^2$ (Einstein)	Nuclear Energy
Attraction (So many "discoverers" ...)	Endless Proof

The natural law of Attraction has been "discovered", spoken of, written about and taught for centuries. It is at work everyday, in your life now. You can harness the properties of the law of Attraction in order that the things you want can materialize or manifest in your life *more* often, by re-training your thoughts. Conversely, you can harness the properties of law of Attraction in order that the things you do not want can materialize or manifest in your life *less* often, by re-training you thoughts.

Retraining your thoughts, and guiding your own vibrations or feelings, is the same thing. It will take some time, some commitment, and some reminding yourself, in order to change the current thought patterns you have, which are bringing you "the stuff you do not want". All successful people control their vibrations, or "feelings", to their advantage, by controlling their thoughts more effectively than less successful people do. They may not even realize they are doing it. It is possible they have never heard of the law of Attraction. Yet somehow, somewhere, they learned to *think correctly* in order to *get what they want*. They learned to use a thinking process which was in fact, Healthy Thinking, powerfully supercharging their Energy System.

Recap Chapter 4: ENERGIZE

- Deliberately experiencing good feelings about a desire will begin to move that thing towards you.

- The problem with all negative thought or spoken words is that *Attraction does not differentiate between negative or positive, it simply brings you what you think about.* Stay focused on what you *want*.

- Successful leaders *say the words* that others hesitate to say.

- You will speed up the process of Attraction in direct proportion to the amount of good feelings you have, as you repeatedly think about your desires

- Create your own unique Energy System built of components or strategies to access all 5 senses

- Your goal in the Energize Step is to give attention, energy and focus to your desire

- Always use positive statements about your desires

Questions & Ideas

Chapter 5

KNOWING

~ ~

Beyond
positive
thinking ...

What Now?

OK. You are now using both steps in the Attraction process:

<u>Step 1</u>: You have Decided what you want.
<u>Step 2</u>: You are Energizing your desire.

Do you need to do something additional to *manifest* your desire, or *attract* it? No. What are truly successful people doing that is radically different from everyone else? There is one more element *within* the equation: *Knowing*. Rather than complicating matters by thinking of *Knowing* as a "3rd separate step" that you have to keep remembering to "do", you will benefit greatly by understanding the following. *Knowing is in fact an essential element that needs to be present simultaneously with the Desire and Energize steps.* Decide Energize and *Know* flow together, simply, in your mind. The human brain does not "work" in linear fashion. Your mind does not think sequentially unless you are encouraging it to, by deliberate thought. Instead of thinking of Desire, Energize and *Know* like three steps you must perform sequentially to "get it right", think of the process like this:

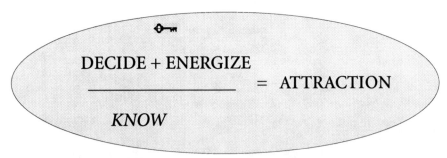

$$\frac{\text{DECIDE} + \text{ENERGIZE}}{KNOW} = \text{ATTRACTION}$$

Knowing is simply the *support* to Decide and Energize. *Knowing* is *allowing* Attraction to bring you your desire by getting the *"I just knew it would happen"* feeling … or the *"I'm going to leave it up to the law of Attraction"* feeling. Knowing is what differentiates *positive thinking* from *the application of the law of Attraction*. It is *Beyond Positive Thinking*. In fact, like the functioning of your mind, the natural law of Attraction does not work in a linear process, but rather through a wonderful, fluid, simple process. There is "no math involved". There is no "do this" *plus* "do this" *plus* "do this" for you to worry about. *It is simply a matter of Deciding what your desire is, and Energizing it, while enjoying the feeling of Knowing it is on its way … all the time.*

Allow = *KNOW*

In other readings about positive thinking or the law Attraction, you may have found the term "allow" used frequently. If you are like many, the term *"allow"* has a bit of a "Huh?" factor, and leaves many people scratching their heads in confusion. However, it is correct and absolutely foolproof, that:

> ✦━ *Whatever you truly desire, and repeatedly think about, with simultaneous good feelings, will eventually come to you.* The simultaneous good feelings *must include a Knowing that your desire is on the way.*

Knowing: This is what is meant by "allowing it", or "releasing". In order to attract the good things you want into your life, you must enable your servant brain to <u>*Know*</u> your desire is "en route", or to expect it, thus mentally paving the way for its arrival. The term "allow" is difficult for some of us to "feel". It is difficult to apply in the business world. We are not used to saying "I just *allowed* it and it appeared!" However … we *are* used to saying "I just *knew* this would happen!" Can you feel the difference?

Another way to interpret *Knowing*, which some may find feels right for them, is the concept of *letting go*. Though the term "letting go" has a bit of a "new age" feel to it, there is truth to the fact that the more you relax about your desire, once you have Decided and Energized it, the more quickly it will manifest. Always. In other words the term "letting go", is the same as *relaxing* about it all. When we are relaxed about something, we have no doubt about it, no fear about it and no negative feelings about it whatsoever.

✦━
Thankfully, *Knowing* also means that you do not have to constantly be *working* on your desires. After all, you *Know* they will materialize, so you can simply relax about it all … *let Attraction "figure it out".*

Most people are more familiar, more comfortable and more "in sync" with the term *Know* than the term *allow.* The term *Knowing* is more suited to the business world as well.

The "parts" you use to build your Energy System should be effective at Energizing your desire in any way that gets *you feeling that your desire is on its way now, or what it would actually feel like to have it.* The more often you get that feeling and the longer you hold it, the faster Attraction delivers your desire. Repeat exercises and activities that give you that good feeling over, and over, and over.

Proof Note: Winning a Home

Two of my very special friends are "real" winners. They won beautiful luxury homes in charity lotteries. Here is Trish's story.

Trish is a beautiful, warm and fun loving person, busy raising her children on her own, while living in an apartment for seven years. Her father, whom she was very close to, died suddenly, leaving her missing him as only a truly beloved daughter can. Shortly afterwards, Trish bought a $100 ticket for a luxury home. At the moment of the purchase, a friend was with her, when a butterfly landed on Trish's arm. She felt this was a sign from her father that she would win the home, and excitedly exclaimed her feelings to her friend. She also bravely told others, including her mother.

Trish constantly had the feeling that she *knew* she would win the home. Of course, she *did* win. She is now enjoying her new 5000 square foot home, complete with her favourite room, the theatre suite, in a beautiful neighbourhood.

The point is, that *how* you get the *Knowing* feeling is irrelevant. It is simply natural law, that once you *have* that feeling, your heart's desire will materialize. Attraction has no option but to bring it to you.

Still Think "It" Can't Happen to You?

An effective tool in fortifying your own resolve that you *can* have more of what you want, is to prove to yourself that others have already achieved the same types of goals. Proving this is possible will help you remove doubt and replace it with *Knowing*.

Here is some proof to think about when doubt rears its ugly head:

- ✓ Billions of other people everywhere have good relationships, and fine things. You deserve the same.

✓ Many other people are doing exactly what they want to do every day. You deserve to be doing what you want in your day-to-day occupation and activities as well.

✓ Other people everywhere are relaxing daily. You deserve to be relaxing as well.

✓ Millions of other people have attained and maintained their ideal weight and fitness level. You can too.

✓ Many other people obtain everything they require in life, without unmanageable stress. You deserve to have whatever you require in life without constant struggle. Life can be much easier and much more fun.

✓ Millions of others have started with nothing, and developed new careers and successful businesses. You can do the same.

As with the countless people who have succeeded before you, in the pursuit of their dreams, you can do the same. What you need to do is incorporate Decide Energize and *Know* into how you think and act. Less of what you do *not* want and *more* of what you *truly want* will then manifest.

Starter Statement

You can immediately apply the basic concept in a "Starter Statement". (In Chapter 6, you will learn to create and use your own unique "A" Statements. These are powerful, simple and effective tools for your Energy System.) The following Starter Statement Exercise will help you begin to create statements that feel and are true for you. Your new statements will help you remove doubt and replace it with *Knowing*.

Exercise # 8. Starter Statement

Fill in the blanks in squares 3 & 4 with a statement about your desire. The statement must feel true to you. Re-read, think about, or say your Starter Statement frequently.

1 Example (*Desire: finding true love*): *Fact:* Others have <u>found their ideal life partner</u>.	2 <u>Starter Statement</u> I know <u>I will find my ideal life partner</u> as well.
3 Your Desire:_____ *Fact:* Others have _____ _____ .	4 <u>Your Starter Statement</u> I know I will _____ _____ .

The above is a Starter Statement to help you begin to shift your incorrect beliefs. You will master this effective and motivating tool later with "A Statements". Many people have unknowingly convinced themselves that certain lies are truths. Have you ever heard statements like "It is more likely that a single woman over 40 gets hit by lightening, than it is that she finds true love?" Or how about "The rich get richer and the poor get poorer." These are incorrect generalities and lies that do *not* apply to us as individuals. There are millions of people who have done the opposite of what those types of statements are telling us. It can happen to you.

But How!!???!????

The feeling of *Knowing that your desire is on its way* is a good feeling you *have had before*. It feels very Healthy. You have had this feeling when you have been about to experience something pleasant or perhaps extraordinary. You have felt it when you have had faith that everything would work out. You experienced it when something good happened to you, and in retrospect, you said, "I just *knew* it!" *Knowing is an element of Healthy Thinking.*

Examples

1.   You are about to give your loved one a special birthday gift she or he really wants, yet did not think you could find. But you did find it. You feel the excitement as your beloved spouse is about to open the gift. You *know* what is about to happen. You know the good feeling you both will experience.

2.   You have purchased a fundraising raffle ticket and as the draw takes place, for some reason, *you just know* you will be the winner.

3.   Your child has been studying regularly, getting good grades and generally enjoying school. You have no doubt she will succeed and be promoted to the next grade.

4.   You have strong spiritual beliefs and regularly pray for answers to problems. You know that your answers always come, whenever you have strongly felt faith that your prayers will be answered.

5.   As your company enters into the fourth quarter, you have a gut feeling that sales will sky rocket. And sure enough, they do.

What is the difference between examples 1, 2, 3, 4 and 5 above, and instances when the opposite outcome is the case? In our examples, "you" allowed only the *knowing* feeling into your thinking about the outcome. If "you" would have allowed in the doubt feeling, what do you think the result would be? You get *what you allow yourself to feel.*

The feeling of *Knowing*, or allowing, is *the lack of doubt.*
It is the Attraction "ignition key". You get *what you
allow yourself to feel.*

Know is the Ignition Key

Think of the Decide step as the brand new car. Think of the Energize step as
the tank full of fuel. Think of *Knowing* as the key that starts the engine. As long
as the key is in the ignition, and turned on, the car is running.

Knowing. Allowing. Faith. Confidence. Belief. Lack of Doubt. It's all the same
thing! *Knowing* attracts the desire that you have Decided upon and Energized,
every time.

BA: Top business leaders and sports athletes use techniques that are radically
different from their peers. They remain totally focused on the target or object
of their desire, sometimes in a state other would consider "extreme stress".
Contrary to what others may assume, some do not use 7-step programs, goal
setting, visualization, or meditation at all. What they are experiencing is a re-
framing strategy of one type or another that includes setting all other issues
aside and a deep *Knowing*.

Society Fosters Doubt

Be kind to yourself as you discover the limiting beliefs or doubts within you.
Though these are obstacles to the manifesting of your desires, know that you
did not put them there. The societies, families and circumstances we live in
did. Most of us constantly receive negative messages, or words which create
negative feelings or vibrations within us, sometimes from the time we are
born. Until we as a human race correct the negative systems we bring children
into, the struggle will continue. Now however, more and more people are talking about the law of Attraction, which has always existed, yet was not widely
known for what it truly is. It is a simple, powerful, Healthy way of thinking. It
is a natural law, as powerful, irrefutable and unwavering as Gravity itself. It is
the eternally present system for *asking and receiving*, available to all, regardless
of race, colour or creed.

Removing All Doubt

It is of utmost importance that you begin to eliminate all doubt pertaining to your fondest wishes, as this doubt is cancelling out your desires! You *can* do this, and you *have* done it many times before, by simply Deciding. Now you will learn to do it deliberately. And watch what happens.

When you first Decide on something you really want, it is typical to get a strong "Knowing" vibration. When you initially begin applying Attraction deliberately, to a desire you have, this can be an exciting, exhilarating feeling, often combined with a strong desire to tell someone. Some people compare it to finding true love. You just *Know* great things are going to happen, and you will have what you want! It is also normal to have vacillating feelings and vibrations throughout the process, when doubt rears its ugly head. However, you now have a system … weapons … to conquer the demon of doubt … your Energy System. You can protect yourself … you can protect your dreams. Your "job" is to control your thoughts and vibrations and to keep yourself feeling confidently content that your desire is on the way or feeling "as if it is already here".

BA: Business leaders and entrepreneurs know this feeling very well. Search any bookstore business section, and you will find countless examples of these leaders, and their use of good, positive, confident feelings in the pursuit of their goals. From Alexander Graham Bell to Mary Kay Ash, to Marie Curie to the Google people … their dream, desire, goal, or big idea, was firmly rooted in their minds as a *known* path to success. They had little, or even *zero* doubt.

Why is "Knowing" so Powerful?

We are getting exactly **what matches the feelings** or vibrations we are sending out.

Yes, it is true … whether we want to admit it or not, we are getting exactly what matches *the feelings* or vibrations we are emitting. Therefore, we want to be better at putting out positive feelings, vibrations, thoughts and moods … attached or in relation to our desires.

Doubt, fear, and expecting disappointment, are all viruses in the computer that is your brain. They are power outages to the movie projector in your mind. They are the "E" light on your gas gauge. As you get better at controlling these vibrations, moods and feelings, your life will gradually improve. You have attracted undesirable elements into your life with these negative vibrations or thoughts *already*. Remember, the law of Attraction brings you what you think about repeatedly, especially if you are infusing your thought with strong emotion. Have you ever heard the phrase "Your worst fears come true"? This is correct. *Therefore, your job is to Know <u>your desires</u> will come true instead.* Your work in Attraction is to keep your thinking process about your desire *feeling good*, feeling like your desire is on the way … *or already here.*

"How Long Will All This Take?"

It is well known that the *removal* of doubt, or *Knowing*, speeds up the manifestation of desires exponentially. How long the manifestation will take, for each individual, and for each differing desire is unknown. You will know you are moving in the right direction as your thoughts become aligned with your desire. Little by little, degree by degree, your thoughts will correct and you will feel better about your life in general. This is a strong indication that you are "getting it". You are beginning to remove doubt. Keep going. Continue that type of thought "tweaking", re-focus and correcting, with each of your desires. Some things that we apply our focus, energy and attention to, manifest very rapidly, even the same day, or the next. *Some things, and especially major desires, can take more time, since we may have a significant amount of doubt to eliminate first.* After all, if you had no doubt about it, and if that had been your frame of mind for a significant amount of time, your desire would already have been delivered to you by the law of Attraction. Sometimes … something even better shows up ☺

Millions of people, right now, are already skilled at using Decide Energize/*Know*, are already attracting what they want, and are already enjoying an abundant joyful life. You can too.

Learning to *Know*

You can eventually become an expert at Attraction. Deciding, Energizing while *Knowing* can be part of your *way of living*, enabling you to deliberately create your ideal life. To become skilled in this process is in fact *easy*. No one is claiming that creating your ideal life will happen like magic … yet the process is amazingly simple. It requires you to deliberately take control of your thoughts and re-direct them. Period. Over and over again. It is simple, yet requires repetition and commitment. It is not complex. It is simply a matter of learning something new. You have learned a million new things since you were born. You can learn *this* new thing as well.

○─┅

All of us, even those of us who are more accustomed to deliberately creating, need to stay focused, and apply Healthy Thinking in order to keep our Energy System in tiptop form. That way, we attract more of what we want and less and less of what we do not want.

The Exercises you are learning can keep you on track, to help you to get, or maintain, the *Knowing* feeling. Practice each of them in order to get a feel for how and when they will be useful to you, in your day-to-day life.

Just as you did when you learned to walk, play ball ride a bicycle or sew, the first few times you use the Restart Exercise, you may feel a little awkward. That's OK. Stay with it. It will eventually become a powerful tool in your arsenal of *Knowing*. This exercise is especially useful when you are in a bad mood, have gone from *feeling good*, to something else, and are effectively attracting stuff you really do *not* want.

Example: You are having a good day. Positive thoughts, including some about your desires and goals, are on your mind. The achievement of an important goal has been playing on and off in your mind like a movie scene. There's a spring in your step. Then … someone at work, or at home, bursts your bubble with his or her negative vibration. This is the perfect time to use the Restart Exercise.

Exercise # 9. <u>Restart</u>

<u>Step 1</u>: Stop whatever you are doing as soon as you possibly can. Head for the bathroom, bedroom or spare room, library carol, outdoors for a walk, any place where you can concentrate alone. You are about to take an Attraction break and restart the computer that is running your "Decide Energize *Know*" Energy System.

<u>Step 2</u>: Take deep relaxing breaths while you do the following. Close your eyes if possible and begin to think about your desires. Play your thoughts out like a movie in your mind, or in written script running across your mind like a screen saver. You are imagining the desires already here. You have it. You are experiencing it. You can see yourself in the scene of this new enjoyable experience you deserve. When your mind wanders, just bring it back to your movie scene. Do this for 30 to 60 seconds.

Note: if you have a visual cue handy, you could look at it while you are Restarting. If you prefer a sound cue, and are able to access one, do so.

<u>Step 3:</u> Smile. ☺ Yes, that's right. Smile, while you take 3 relaxing deep breaths, holding your desire in your mind.

Note: Research shows that the act of smiling, which uses several muscles, releases endorphins in your brain, creating the *feeling of happiness*. Endorphins are naturally occurring chemicals in our brain, which trigger pleasant feelings. You are *always* aiming to Energize your desires with feelings of happiness. Adding smiles to your Exercises will act as an Energy System booster.

Let's Get Physical

Physical exercise is a powerful method to change one's mood, feeling, or frame of mind. Exercising changes the body chemistry to supercharge it with endorphins. In health care, patients with clinical depression are counselled to include exercise in their rehabilitation programs. The successful use of physical exercise in mental well-being is well documented.

BA: Success-oriented companies and organizations are now including wellness and exercise programs in the workplace. Evidence now shows these organizations will fare better than their competitors in attaining their production and service goals, not to mention a healthier bottom line.

Choose whatever physical activity you enjoy for the following powerful *Knowing* exercise. Dancing, for example, might be perfect for you, while walking may be right for another. For those of you who use a wheelchair for mobilization, you can use upper body exercise. You can alternate with various types of exercise from one time to another. You may want to play some dance music, rock, or jazz while you enjoy this one.

Exercise # 10. Exercise!

Step 1: Take 3 deep relaxing breaths while focusing on a visual desire cue, such as a picture, or the picture you have in your mind. With each breath in, raise your arms high, then lower them as you exhale.

Step 2: Keep your desire in your mind, while you exercise or dance for 5 to 15 minutes. You may build up to 15 minutes if you like, starting with just one minute. One minute is better than none, and one good minute of focus on your desire is very powerful indeed. Whenever your mind wanders, bring it back to your desire.

Note: Using verbal "out loud" statements about your desire while exercising, is another "booster" to this exercise.

Example: "I love the fact that my _____is on its way to me now." Say it with feeling, acting really excited while you say it. Pretend if you have to.

Exercise #10 is especially useful for
Energizing your desires in the area of Health. For example, if you want a stronger more muscular body, or more flexibility, these goals can be effectively Energized using this Exercise.

Find Evidence

Finding evidence that what you want *is* possible will help you accept or *Know* that it is on the way to you. Having evidence about a fact enables our brain to accept it as true. This applies in all fields of study. For example, scientists and clinical researchers are satisfied only when they find evidence of a theory being "true" … usually multiple examples of this. They are only satisfied that something is "the way it seems", or "the way we think it is", once they find proof. They agree that "something works like we think it should", only when they have evidence. Once they *Know* a thing for sure, they are satisfied, and the discovery may find its way into common usage.

Knowing and Believing

You may be wondering, "Do I have to *believe* in the law of Attraction for it to work?" **No.** Let us review the following definitions:

Theory: an idea someone has that something works in a particular way.
Example: There may be life on Mars.

Belief: by repetitive thought, or by assuming a statement made by another is true, one comes to believe a thing to be true.
Example: "I can't become a physicist, because my father always said I was not smart enough."

Knowing: beyond a theory, beyond simply believing, you <u>*Know*</u> a thing to be true, because there is evidence. There is evidence that it could happen to you.
Example: A Mother views the Helen Keller movie. Her child is blind and deaf as well. She now *knows* her child can accomplish great things despite the limitations present.

When you *Know* something is
possible, you are unstoppable.

<u>Remember:</u>

The key to attracting what you want, or something better, is that
whatever you repeatedly think about, with simultaneous good feelings*,
will eventually come to you.
That's it. It is Law. It is irrefutable.
It is at work in every molecule of the Universe.
*The <u>*simultaneous good feelings*</u> include *Knowing* your desire is on its way to
you now.

You asked, "Do I have to *believe* in the law of Attraction for it to work?" The
answer to that question is "No". You do not have to believe in Attraction any
more than you have to believe in Gravity. They are both already and always at
work in your life. You are already getting exactly what you are feeling and
vibrating. If you throw a ball, it will eventually hit the ground … whether you
believe in the natural law of Gravity or not.

Who Do You Think You Are?

The following exercise will silence the negative voice in your head that up until
now, may have been saying, "*Who do you think you are? You can't have that!*"
This is a fun research project. You will continue it for weeks, and maybe longer.
You are about to create a list which will enable you to remove all doubt that
you can have your desire, by finding evidence. You will be keeping this list, so
you should use a notebook you can purchase from stationary, department or
dollar stores.

Exercise # 11. <u>Birds of a Feather</u>

<u>Title your List</u>: "<u>If These People Can Do It, So Can I!</u>"

<u>Conduct your Research:</u> Using the Internet, books in the Public Library, your kids' schoolbooks, newspapers, news programs, documentaries and movies, begin seeking out your "Birds of a Feather". Look for stories of people who have achieved the same types of goals or desires you have. Look for those who came from similar backgrounds or starting points. Look for those who came from much more difficult beginnings. Look for individuals from any nation or background. Look for accomplishers of great things, and of small things.

Continue to build your list. Number the individuals. You will soon see that others have done what you are seeking to do, as well as more difficult and "impossible" things.

Make a note or asterix beside those whose story has particular meaning or interest for you. You may want to do further reading later.

Use this list and review it when you need a "Knowing boost."

Once you remove doubt, your desire will materialize.
It is law.

Your Personal Attraction Partners ☺+☺

Have you ever had an idea or interest that flourished because you sought out like-minded individuals? Human beings are programmed to communicate, commiserate, bond, join forces and generally "hang out". We accomplish massive and seemingly unattainable goals by working together and by getting excited about new ideas together. One of your most effective strategies for removing doubt and allowing Attraction to improve your life is that of finding and communicating with like-minded individuals … other positive thinkers who have recognized Attraction at work in their lives.

People who are open to the idea of the law of Attraction probably already exist in your life. If not, you could attract them to you … you simply need to apply Decide Energize while *Knowing,* to that desire.

If someone you know introduced you to the concept of Attraction, then you already have an Attraction partner or like-minded friend to start with. It only takes one. More will appear as time goes on, if you desire it.

Why is a Partner Important?

You will enjoy (get good *feelings*) comparing stories and Attraction events happening in each of your lives. The interesting side effect of all this commiserating is that manifestations will multiply as well as speed up! Having someone to share with will enable you to remove doubt, and attract your desires by *Knowing* that the law of Attraction works. *Finding and discussing "proof" is a powerful tool for Knowing, and therefore attracting.* It strengthens the *"Knowing"* components of your Energy System. It works. Period.

If you already have an Attraction partner, great! Now make it a point to talk to each other at least once a week, about the progress each of you is making. You will find more and more to talk about.

Example of subjects to discuss:

- Something you attracted, recently or even a long time ago, and "how"
- Someone significant, who has appeared in your life
- A business success you are now enjoying, and how you attracted it
- Evidence or co-incidences: you will notice more and more of those.
- Books and articles you are reading or have heard about
- Movies that involve a Positive Thinking or Attraction theme
- Internet sites that are "in sync" with LOA

- ⚷ New Attraction tools and strategies you are using
- ⚷ Events, things and people you are Attracting now
- ⚷ "Funny things that happened on the way to …"
- ⚷ Positive organizational changes now happening in your workplace
- ⚷ Decisions you have made in order to create the life you want

The Masters are Your Partners

Find works by the masters of the natural law of Attraction. CDs, Videos, old cassette tapes, books, articles … there is an abundance of tools, there for the asking, for you to tap into. Many great teachers have inspired millions to change their lives through the basic techniques of Decide Energize *Know*. The vocabulary, or terminology, may have been different, but the concepts remain the same. You may not be able to have a verbal "here and now" conversation with these enlightened souls, but you can hear their voices, and learn their lessons through their works. They will inspire you and re-enforce your *Knowing* that your desire is on its way to you now.

BA: Successful business leaders, many of whom prefer to remain private about their readings and personal success strategies, are voracious readers and explorers of biographies and success resources about, or created by, the masters of Attraction.

Remember:

- ⚷ Once you have the *feeling* that you *Know* you can have your desire … your desire is on its way. It is Law.
- ⚷ Attraction partners will help you feel the good vibration of *Knowing*, and your desires will follow.
- ⚷ The faster you remove all doubt, the faster you allow your desire to materialize

The Story of James 🗍

The following story will highlight how effective the *Knowing* element is, even in difficult situations, attracting a desired outcome.

Part 1: James, 10 years old, grew up in a dysfunctional home, where his alcoholic parents told him he would never be able to go to college. He loves animals, and has a child's wish to become a veterinarian. Unfortunately, until now, he believes his parents, and does poorly in school.

Part 2: James is now 14. His desire to become a veterinarian remains, seemingly dormant. One day, at a friend's house, he watches the movie "The Incredible Journey©", about two dogs and a cat who are lost, yet survive against all odds. His desire begins to take root. He cannot stop thinking about it. "Out of the blue", a veterinarian shows up as the guest speaker in his classroom. The veterinarian is an African-American who grew up in the ghetto. James begins to think that "maybe … just maybe" … and so his desire grows. The doubt in his mind is being pushed out by *Knowing*. His grades skyrocket.

Part 3: Having earned a full scholarship, James is in his 1st year of Veterinary College. There is no doubt in anyone's mind, including his own, that he will graduate.

Part 4: In his 4th year, James is finding the curriculum easy and enjoyable, and takes extra courses. He graduates one year ahead of schedule.

Let us analyse James' story.

The Story of James	Analysis
James, 10 years old, grew up in a dysfunctional home where his alcoholic parents told him he would never be able to go to college.	James is in troubled situation … bad vibes, negative feelings, unpredictability. Many people start out life like this. Studies are showing that the percentage of children growing up in dysfunctional homes is staggering.
He loves animals, and has a child's wish to become a veterinarian.	All human beings, even small children and babies, have desires, wishes, dreams and goals. It is a powerful drive within all of us.
Unfortunately, until now, he believes his parents, and does poorly in school.	Strong doubt = desire *not* manifesting James is overwhelmed by the negative feelings or vibrations he is subjected to constantly, resulting in poor grades.
James is now 14. His desire to become a veterinarian remains, seemingly dormant. One day, at a friend's house, he watches the movie "The Incredible Journey©", about 2 dogs and a cat who are lost, yet survive against all odds. His desire begins to take root. He cannot stop thinking about it.	James has always continued thinking about his desire. LOA is bringing him more of what he thinks about. The power of his wonderful dream is growing.
"Out of the blue", a veterinarian shows up as the guest speaker in his classroom. The veterinarian is an African-American who grew up in the ghetto. James begins to think that "maybe … just maybe" … and so his desire grows. The doubt in his mind is being pushed out by *Knowing*. His grades skyrocket	Weakened doubt = desire *beginning to mobilize* towards James Unknowingly, or by default, James has attracted the veterinarian, a "classic" manifestation of Attraction at work. His desire is now a force to reckon with. He is unstoppable.
Having earned a full scholarship, James is in his 1st year of Veterinary college. There is no doubt in anyone's mind, including his own, that he will graduate.	Zero doubt = desire *manifesting* *Knowing* his desire is on the way, all manner of things, people and events manifest for James, and his desire materializes quickly.
In his 4th year, James is finding the curriculum easy and enjoyable, and takes extra courses. He graduates one year ahead of schedule.	Continuous zero doubt = *Speedy* manifestation of desire

James' is a typical "Against All Odds" story. Every person on earth with a similar story has attracted what he or she desired by virtue of the *Knowing* element of the natural law of Attraction. How much doubt do you have? How quickly do you want your desire to materialize? Is it worth putting some commitment and Energy into the project?

Strong Doubt = Desire Not Manifesting

Weakened Doubt = Desire Beginning to Mobilize

Continuous Zero Doubt = Desires Manifests Fast

Moving Towards

Of course, it is natural and important to always move *in the direction of* your goal, your desires, the things, people and events you want more of. Taking action in the direction *opposite* to your desires will bring you more of the things, people and events you do not want.

You & Your #1 Attraction Partner: Together you are Unstoppable

Ideally, you want your spouse, or your best friend, to be part of your Attraction "crew". If you are not in such a relationship at this time, *use Attraction to attract one.* LOA can attract into your life a better relationship with your family members, as well as new friends. It is wonderful to have someone with whom you can share experiences, co-incidences and stories, as well as to just *have fun with* on this new Healthy Thinking level. At first, it may be that your "new attitude" is met with "them looking at you funny". However, everyone has goals, dreams, desires and "*Whatever's*" that they want more of. When your friends and loved ones see your life improving, and all manner of good things coming to you, they will surely wonder, and may begin to ask you questions.

Not Your Job

It is not your "job" to change anyone else's mind or anyone else's life. *It is your "job" to attract what you want into your life.* Energize your desires and the changes will follow. Trying to "convert" people is not part of LOA. Just be yourself. Just enjoy the manifestations … acknowledge and appreciate it all. Others are following *their* dreams, in some way. You are only responsible for your own feelings, vibrations, desires and manifestations.

This Is Your Job

O—¬
Your work, or *job*, in applying Attraction, is to keep your thinking process about *your* desires Healthy and feeling *good*. Keep your Energy System working for you.

How Will I Know I Am Doing This Right?

Some people find it easy to Decide what they want, and simple to Energize that desire, yet think they do not have the *Know* part right. Unfortunately, if they *think* they don't have it right, of course, they *are* right about *that*! That is simply how Attraction works!

First, you will know you have Attraction "figured out" by the changes that begin to show up in your life or business. Things, people and events you have been thinking about will materialize. Co-incidences (or instances of evidence) will multiply. New ideas to achieve your goals will come to mind. People will show up, and in some way, contribute to you attracting what you want. Sometimes your desires will take a period of time to appear. Sometimes your desires will materialize quickly. That is when you know you have summoned the law of Attraction and in perfect harmony with it, created something *deliberately*.

Note: Thankfully, most desires do not appear the instant you think of them. There is a time lapse involved. This gives you time to modify, tweak and clarify your desires to ensure you get what you *really* want. Most importantly, in retrospect, you will be grateful that some desires you were hoping for at some point in the past did *not* materialize.

<u>Secondly</u>, you will also know you "have it figured out" by the general improvement in your moods, feelings and outlook on life. Hope will be a more common feeling. Your general outlook on life will be more positive. This is Healthy Thinking. You will experience a feeling or vibration of relief from frustration, hopelessness, boredom and worry. Frequently, while you are simply doing deliberate Attraction exercises or consciously Deciding, you will feel relief from a not-so-pleasant feeling you were experiencing. It is Healthy Thinking at work for you.

The following is a typical example I experienced: the *Knowing* factor was at work, and Attraction orchestrated whatever needed to happen to manifest the desire.

Proof Note: Meeting The Anchor

I was attending an annual convention, an event where over 8,000 people gather yearly to work on improving the health care system. The agenda included a presentation by a famous and respected news anchor. I will call him Richard. I had admired him for years, since the late eighties when he was covering the fall of the Berlin wall. The world was glued to the television for this historic and joyous event, and as usual, he always knew exactly what to say to make us feel like we were part of it all.

I began to think … hmmm … I would like to meet Richard. I thought about perhaps getting his autograph. In my visual thoughts was a "piece of paper" exchanged between us. I did not really spend much time thinking about it, and I am not "into" autographs. Yet somehow … I just *knew* I would end up meeting him.

The night before he was to speak, I was having dinner at my cousin Paul & his partner Dave's home. I was telling them about the line up of speakers this year, and mentioned Richard. Paul got up, asked me to follow him over to a large framed photo on the wall. He said, "Maybe you could give him a copy of this." It was a beautiful early 1900's sepia photo of a large family … *Richard's family* … with his grandfather as a little boy in it! "What's this all about?" I asked, quite baffled. As it turns out, Richard's grandfather was related to my Cousin Paul's aunt, on his "other side" … the side I never knew. Paul and I are the same age, and as children, our families visited frequently. We always kept in touch, but I had never heard of the "Richard connection".

Dave scanned a large, beautiful copy for me, and Paul jotted down all the names and dates on the outside of the envelope, as well as his own email address.

I had the envelope with me as the conference room filled with over 2,000 people. I was chatting with colleagues and told them my story, but was intimidated and hesitant about trying to meet the famous Richard. I spotted some conference staff at the front—too far from where I was to recognize anyone. I made my way over to them, thinking I would have one of them give Richard the photo after the presentation. One of them recognized me, from previous health care meetings or presentations I had done, and greeted me warmly. Hoping they would relay it for me, I was quickly telling them the story while showing the antique photo. They not only insisted I give it to Richard myself, but they quickly "elbowed" me onto the stage where Richard was getting ready to speak! Nervous and uncomfortable, as I did not want to seem like a crazed fan, I introduced myself, we shook hands, and I gave him the picture with a quick explanation. He greeted me warmly, and was very grateful. And to top it off, he later made contact with my cousin Paul via email to express his gratitude!

Doubt Zingers

As you begin to use Healthy Thinking, and your general attitude becomes more and more positive, others may comment. As your vocabulary loses its PWs, and transforms into a more optimistic, goal-focused style, people may wonder what is different about you, especially if you were previously quite negative or pessimistic. You may even encounter the occasional "glass is half empty" person who tries to burst your bubble, and remind you that something bad is bound to happen next, or tell you that all this Attraction stuff is just new age mumbo jumbo. Here are a few suggestions to protect yourself from the Doubt Zingers:

Doubt Zinger:	You say:
"Nothing will ever change in this workplace! You're wasting your time."	"I appreciate your concern for me. Let's have coffee and re-visit this topic this time next year." Smile and change the subject or walk away.
"You seem a little too cheerful, what's up with you?"	"Quite a few things are going my way lately. Thanks for asking."
"You'll see ... the bottom will fall out soon ..."	"Thanks for thinking about me. I do have a safety net. Hey! I like that new shirt you're wearing. Where did you get it?"
"I saw you were reading that Attraction stuff. I hope you don't believe in that!"	"Thanks for your concern. There is no believing involved, actually. It's all about Healthy Thinking." If the person really is interested, they can do their own research ... refer them to Earl Nightingale, Catherine Ponder or another favourite of yours. It is not your job to convert anyone.

The point is that *they* are in the process of attracting exactly what *they* are thinking, vibrating, feeling, putting out ... as always. You know what to do. Go back to Decide + Energize/*Know*, and Attract positive supportive interactions for yourself day to day, at home and in the workplace.

Gratitude is Acknowledgement

The law of Attraction is at its most powerful in your life when you are in the habit of recognizing that it is at work. One of the most effective ways to apply the natural law of Attraction and to ensure constant improvement in your life is to *express gratitude, acknowledgement and appreciation about the good things in your life*. Begin to notice and acknowledge the good things, people and events all around you and in your day-to-day life and these will multiply exponentially. This is a wonderful feature of LOA, which will contribute greatly to bringing you more of what you truly want in life.

What you are really doing by acknowledging or noticing the "good stuff", is giving it positive *attention, energy and focus*. And what happens when you do that? You get more of it!

Gratitude and Abundance $$$

Gratitude and abundance have an excellent and powerful relationship. For example, suppose your desire has something to do with more money, sales, and a higher income or zero debt. By *noticing or observing* the abundance all around you, you are creating a good feeling or sending out positive vibrations. These are feelings of gratitude. Noticing a good thing in your life is the same feeling as the "thank you" feeling. If we were to measure the "noticing" feeling, or vibration, it would surely rate equal or close to the "gratitude" vibration. By noticing the abundance already in your life, you will begin to receive more of whatever you are noticing!

Now what normally happens when you do something good for someone and they don't even seem to notice? You *may* do it again, *once or twice*. However, if that someone continues to ignore your gesture, never acknowledges it, or never says "thank you", will you continue doing it? Attraction works in the same way as we do. When we express gratitude or acknowledgment of the good things in our life, Attraction sends us more!

Start noticing a particular thing and more shows up. Start acknowledging it by consciously paying attention to its appearance, and it will *really* show up. Start expressing your gratitude, your acknowledgement or your "noticing of it", and WOW! Stand back.

Ways to Express Gratitude

We spend much of our time so busy and pre-occupied with our work, families and the stresses of living in the 21st century, that we rarely stop to smell the roses. You will benefit from good feelings, and the ability to *Know* your desires are manifesting, when you are in the regular habit of noticing the good and abundant things around you. Incorporate this type of thought process in your day-to-day life, and you will have immediate benefits.

Suggested ways to observe and acknowledge abundance:

- Notice the abundance of transportation methods in our modern societies—how many do you have access to when you really stop to think about it?
- How did this book come into your hands? What resources materialized in order for you to enjoy the experience of reading it?
- What are the natural and fabricated surroundings you see every day? What did it take for all this to grow, or be constructed? Are you or your company benefiting in any way from their existence?
- Is there a store near you where you could purchase food? Are the shelves well stocked?
- If you had personal difficulties, are there people who could help you in your area? Friends? Family? A counsellor? A business owner? A physician or other health care professional? A clergy person or spiritual counsellor?
- Notice the abundance of dedicated board members, volunteers, employees and loyal clients in your organization
- Observe and comment on the love, kindness and respect people in your life are giving you

Most of us are so overwhelmingly surrounded by an abundance of things, people and resources to which we have access, that we would not be able to list them on 10 sheets of legal paper if we tried.

- The natural law of Attraction responds to your giving attention, energy and focus to all this abundance, and *sends you more.*

Proof Note: Brenda's Earrings

Brenda was one of the Managers on my team and is now enjoying early retirement. A special luncheon had been planned for her, and the purchasing of the gift had caused quite a bit of consternation. What would she really appreciate? She was not known to wear jewellery other than a tiny pair of studs. We were not sure what her home décor and artistic tastes were at this time. However, a lovely and intricate set of gold studs were purchased, and we crossed our fingers hoping she would like them.

Though Brenda has a dynamic personality, we were quite surprised at the level of astonishment she displayed when she opened the box. As it turns out, she had decided that one of her retirement treats to herself was going to be ... jewellery! Not just any jewellery, but very specific items. One of the pieces on her list was *exactly this pair of earrings*, in this size (medium, not the large or small options). She had even gone to a jewellery store and tried them on, planning to purchase them later. When our secret shopper purchased them, at the same store, no mention of the intended recipient was made. We thought that for sure, somehow the storeowner knew the gift was for this particular person, but no, she had no clue.

Brenda's is a perfect example of the 2-step formula: Decide Energize/*Know* = Attraction. She *Decided* she wanted those earrings. She *Energized* the desire by trying them on. She *Knew* she would have them all along, and had Decided to buy them eventually. Instead, the natural law of Attraction sped things up a bit☺ (Something better ...)

<u>You now have the key to</u>
<u>Attracting more of what you want, or something</u>
<u>better, into your life.</u>
Decide what you desire.
Energize your desire by giving it attention.
All the while, ***Know*** that your desire is
on the way.

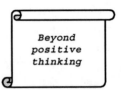

Recap Chapter 5: KNOWING

- Thankfully, *Knowing* also means that you do not have to "constantly be *working*" on your desires. After all, you *Know* they will materialize, so you can simply relax about it all ... *let Attraction "figure it out".*

- The feeling of *Knowing*, or allowing, is *the lack of doubt*. It is the Attraction "ignition key". You get *what you allow yourself to feel.*

- *All of us*, even those of us who are more accustomed to deliberately creating, need to stay focused, and apply Healthy Thinking in order to keep our Energy System in tiptop form.

- When you *Know* something is possible, you are unstoppable.

- Once you remove doubt, your desire will materialize. It is law.

- Your work, or *job*, in applying Attraction, is to keep your thinking process about *your* desires Healthy and *feeling good.*

- What you are really doing by acknowledging or noticing the "good stuff", is giving it positive *attention, energy and focus.* And what happens when you do that? You get more of it!

- It *can* happen to you: think of others who have attracted similar desires

Your job is to eliminate doubt: eliminating doubt is *Knowing*, also termed *allow, or letting go*

Questions & Ideas

Chapter 6

The Power of the Written Word

*I am in the
process of...*

Put It in Writing

Many years ago, when I was going through a particularly trying time, a good friend shared with me a pearl of wisdom which literally changed my life. She was very much in tune with the universe, and perceived as having a bit of the "flower child" in her. She lived in a beautiful home, and enjoyed a beautiful joyful life filled with love and pleasure. In her kind and peaceful way, she passed on a bit of "tried and true" wisdom to her friend. Her words to me were:

"Never underestimate the power of the written word."

Her words were meant to help me get an important message across exactly as I intended it to be. I did not realize at the time, how significant the act of *"scripting"* what I desired was. Following her advice, I proceeded to use "the written word", to clarify what I wanted out of life, in one way or another, on a regular basis.

All manner of information, skills, positive attitude strategies, goal-setting knowledge, teachers, and the "strangest secret" of the law of Attraction, came into my life from that time onward, at a rate I had not yet experienced. Many of the wonderful transformations I enjoyed from that time onward required effort, action and focus. However, many of them seemed to materialize much more easily than I would have thought possible previously. In retrospect, the difference was that *I was now writing down my intentions* about what I wanted.

Are Written Affirmations Working for YOU?

How many of us have tried to improve our lives, or achieve goals, through the process of writing down what are commonly known as "affirmations"? Entire seminars and courses have been given (and many have paid dearly for these), to teach the process and use of affirmations. They were usually taught to sound something like this:

"I am rich." (Even though you may have been poor!)
"I love myself." (Even though you may have been paralysed by negative feelings!)
"I have a wonderful marriage." (Even though you may have been single and had not had a date in years!)

Is it any wonder that for over 80% of us, unfortunately, they just did not work?!

Affirmations like the ones above do not usually work very well. Sometimes they are effective, sometimes they are mildly so, sometimes not at all. They certainly will *not* work, if and when you think or say them, you feel discouragement, disbelief, or negative feelings and vibes of any kind.

However, take heart! All those months and years of re-stating a certain thing you wanted, were not in vain. You *know* there was *something* to the whole affirmation "thing" … it is all about *how* you create and use these statements.

When affirmations do work, it is because of this:
whatever you are saying, or even better, *writing down,*
must *feel true, now,* to you.

Remember: Attraction will bring you what you want when you are experiencing good, *Knowing* feelings about your desire.

"A" Statements Work!

Now let us simplify this whole affirmation business once and for all, with a user-friendly, effective Energizing method anyone can apply.

First, instead of calling these important tools "affirmations", or "desire statements", or even "goal statements", we will simplify things by calling them "*A*" *Statements.* You can think of the "A" component as having whatever significance works for you, at the time.

For example, the "A" could stand for any, some, or all of the following:

- Attraction
- Anything
- A+
- Affirmations

- ⚷ Allow
- ⚷ Amazing
- ⚷ About time!
- ⚷ All Right!!
- ⚷ _____?

Have some fun with this, and relax about whether or not you are "getting it". You do not have to take an affirmation seminar to put Attraction to work for you. Remember: It is all about making *your* Energy System effective for you, so that you can Energize your desires with positive *Knowing* feelings.

<u>Now: create some "A" Statements that will work for *you*.</u>

"A" Statements are at their most powerful when you have *zero doubt* about what you are saying. If you say "I will wake up tomorrow morning 30 years younger.", well … except in fairy tales, no one seems to have succeeded with that one yet. Remember in the previous *Knowing* chapter, when you learned that your desire materializes when all doubt is removed? Remember that finding proof that it *is* possible is important? Has anyone ever done what it is that you want to do? Does anyone else have the same type of thing that you desire? Has anyone ever gotten what it is that *you* want?

There are over 6.5 billion people on the planet. Do you think that maybe, just maybe, one other person has succeeded in a manner similar to the way you intend to?

Now, if you kept thinking, stating, or writing to yourself that "by this time next year, I will look 10 years younger", you absolutely *could* attract that. Why? Because many, many people have already done that. It is not just a matter of determination, luck or buying power. You can actually attract all you need to be, do or have, to look 10 years younger, in one year, even if at this time you can not even afford the cheapest skin cream, and you are 100 pounds overweight. You can attract all you need to be, do or have, in order to look 10 years younger, in one year, even if you have no job and have gone through a nasty divorce. And … the whole process can be easy, enjoyable, and unfold in the most wondrous of ways … attracting all manner of other good stuff to you! Decide, Energize and absolutely *Know* that what you want is on its way, and you will have it. *Writing it down correctly, in an "A" Statement that works for you, will greatly increase the effectiveness of your Energy System.* Here's how:

Example: Fred is 100 pounds overweight. His heart's desire is to be 100 pounds thinner.

Instead of writing and repeating Affirmations like these:	Fred is writing and repeating A Statements like these:
"I have a slim fit muscular body."	"I am in the process of becoming slim, fit and muscular."
"I love the reaction I get when my old friends see me now."	"I love the reaction I will get when my old friends see me in 2 months."
"I am excited about the new clothes I am wearing."	"I am excited about the new clothes I see myself wearing."
"I look awesome in a bathing suit."	"I see myself eventually looking awesome in a bathing suit."
"Women are approaching me every day."	"I am in the process of becoming attractive to more women."
"My team is the top producer in the country."	"My team is in the middle of doubling productivity!"
"Our school has the highest scores in the state/province/country."	"Everyone is thrilled at the climbing scores we are seeing … month after month!"

Have some fun with your "A" Statements and your *scripting*. Did you notice how much different the "A" Statements scripted on the right feel, compared to those on the left of the table? That is because they are believable and true. Fred has no need to "convince himself". In fact, the truth is that *as soon as Fred has clearly Decided on his desire* (to be 100 lbs thinner), with the Energizing and simultaneous *Knowing* he will now apply, he really *is* in the process of attracting his desire.

You can use your "A" Statement in many ways, including simply saying it aloud once a day. Write it on a pocket-sized card! Give yourself permission to desire something wonderful, and Decide to attract it!

Proof Note: Book of "A" Statements

Approximately 7 years ago, I had been researching and studying the works of some of the masters listed at the beginning of this book. I had decided to write down all the events, people and things I wanted in my life, in the form of what

I knew then as "affirmations". Many of these desires were at the time, a long way from the truth I was experiencing. I was successful and moving nicely along a satisfying career path. Life was good, busy and I certainly had little to complain about. However, being human, desires are continuously evolving, and I had quite a long list of wishes.

I purchased a small hard cover journal, with a cover print by Monet, one of my favourite artists. I wrote down many statements about my wishes and goals, as well as affirmations and quotes I found inspiring.

As things, events and positive changes materialized in my life, I tore out those pages ... because they were "taken care of" ... they had manifested! On April 22, 2005, I came across the journal again after not having picked it up for years. I wrote the following: *"Years after writing down many of the first-noted affirmations in this book, to my amazement, so much of it has come to pass! Press on! Press On!"*

There were blank pages still to be filled in the journal, and I am now filling these, scripting the future I intend to have.

The point is this: the traditional "affirmation techniques" we have been taught, *do* work when you can get the *"Knowing"* feeling at the same time as you state the desire.

The Power of Repetition ▶▶▶▶▶

Repeating a thought, or words, over and over, is a powerful tool for your Energy System. It _is_ Healthy to choose good thoughts and good things to strive for, for yourself and for your family, as well as your work or business, and to repeatedly think about those thoughts and words, instead of thinking about what is wrong in your life. Repeating your desires in the form of "A" Statements will create energy (Energize), focus, and help enable the Attraction of your desire.

There is no need to exhaust your brain and force this repetition to occur. The idea is to replace thoughts of things you *do not* want with things you *do* want. This should feel relaxing and enjoyable. This is *not* like your childhood learning experiences, when you were required to memorize or learn by rote. Rather, this is you replacing unpleasant thought with thought about the things you *do* want in your life.

Clarity ☼

Being clear about what you want is a key to attracting it as soon as possible.

"A" Statements help tremendously, simply by the correctness of their form. If you are unclear about what you want, law of Attraction will bring you all kinds of *related* stuff. Think of it like this: when you order a drink, do you have to be clear? Of course! If you just said: "Bring me some kind of drink," who knows what would appear at your table. Attraction works the same way. It requires you to be very specific about what you want.

"A" Statement Examples

What you want, your heart's desire at the center of the thought, is what you need to Attract, is it not? Here are some examples of effective, clear, "A" Statements, in the categories of The Big FOHR. You may want to use these as templates at first.

Remember: the "A" Statement must "ring true" for you—*you must get a good feeling when you say and think it.*

Finances

- "I am applying law of Attraction to my finances and developing a variety of income sources, creating greater and greater cash flow. I can do it!"
- "I am in the process of doubling my take-home income to $__. (*specify amount*) And I love it!"
- "My financial assets are growing, and will reach $___. (*specify amount*). Wow!"
- "I intend to retire in ____years, with $__ (*specify amount*) in savings. Yippee!"
- "I am in the middle of attracting everything I need to be, do and have to attract an ideal finance deal. WooHoo!"
- "I am in the process of attracting a lottery win. The winning has begun!"
- "My debts are manageable and are wonderful tools contributing to the growth of my overall wealth. I am grateful."

Occupation

- "I am in the process of finding the perfect volunteer organization to join. I am so looking forward to helping."
- "I am enjoying changing my part-time occupation into a full-time job. (*or vice versa*) Yahoo!"
- "I am in the process of attracting my new ideal exciting career, of _____. (*specify*) I knew I could do it!"
- "I am attracting everything I need to be, do and have to attract a position at _____ (*specify company*). I'm so excited!"
- "I am getting more and more competent and confident at work every day. I can do it!"
- "I am moving into a career that involves travel to many countries and beautiful places. I can just feel the warm sun on my face."
- "I intend to retire in ___ years. What a fun thing to work on now!"
- "My occupation is becoming more enjoyable and more exciting every day. I love it!"

Health

- "I am getting physically stronger every day. What a great feeling!"
- "I am in the process of reaching my ideal weight of _____. (*specify*) Just thinking of it makes me feel healthy and more attractive!"
- "All manner of events, people and things are aligning for me now, to enable my _____* to disappear. (*pain, tumour, cancer cells, depression, rash, high blood sugar etc …) What a joyful feeling!"
- "I am walking every day now, and soon I will be running! Yay!"
- "I am applying law of Attraction to my life and will pass on in my sleep, in my own home, at the age of 100, after an active and wonderful life on earth. What a peaceful feeling!"
- "My physical and mental health is improving dramatically, and my primary care practitioner is prescribing less and less medication for me. This is great!"

Relationships

- "I am now attracting my ideal spouse. We have so much fun together!"

- "I am getting better and better at parenting my wonderful_____

  (*son/daughter, ___ name*) and he/she is responding with better and better behaviour. I love her/him with all my heart!"

- "I am attracting everything I need to be, do and have to attract my ideal wife/husband/partner/new friend."

- "All manner of events, people and things are aligning for me now, to enable my ideal partner/wife/husband/new friend to appear. I can feel it now!"

- "I am in the middle of attracting a friend to exercise and work out with.

  It feels good to buddy-up with someone."

- "I am in the process of attracting a deeper, more fun, and more satisfying relationship with my husband/partner/wife. We're having a blast!"

The bottom line is this: you will find many variations of "the perfect" A Statement, desire statement or affirmation, depending on what you read and research. *It just simply has to feel good, feel right and feel true for you.*

Clarify Some More ... with Describers

Have some fun with your "A" Statement and put some "Describers" on it.

○━┅
The clearer your thinking process is about the things, people and events you want more of, the easier it is for Attraction to materialize your wishes.

Put some detail into it, to use during your thinking, or meditating. Use all manner of intricate specifications to make it become real for you in your mind. This type of clarity will further power up your Energy System and help you *Know* your desire is on its way.

Use the following Clarity exercise to Energize your "A" Statement.

Exercise # 12. Clarity

<u>Step 1.</u> Write down your "A" Statement while visualizing or imagining it as clearly as you can. Put "your self" in the scene of having your desire or goal, as if it was a scene in a movie.

<u>Step 2.</u> Now write down as many "describers" as you can, and add some feeling to each. Aim for at least 5—10 describers.

Example: Mary has been a couch potato all her life, is 47 pounds overweight and her nurse practitioner has just referred her to the diabetic education program because her blood sugar is consistently high. She knows she has to incorporate exercising into her life, but she has always disliked any form of exercise and prefers sitting and reading quietly with a good smoke. She cannot quite convince herself that she can and will lose 47 pounds.

For now, she has Decided on the following desire, which is on a sticky note all over her house: *"I am walking every day now, and soon I will be running!"*

In her journal, Mary writes down the following Describers:

"I'm kind of excited about walking, and burning off an extra 200 calories a day. That's neat!"
"I think I'll treat myself to really comfortable walking shoes. My toes are smiling just thinking about them ..."
"After every walk I'm going to have a nice shower and a cup of cool peppermint tea. Mmmm ..."
"I'm attracting some really good ideas about where to walk: the park, the track, in a neighbourhood I want to live in ... by the lake ... I'm feeling like walking right now!"

Mary frequently speaks her Describers out loud.

2 weeks later: Mary has lost 5 pounds, her blood sugar is down, and she has a new "A" Statement: "I'm in the process of attracting all I need to be, do or have to get to my ideal weight of 130 pounds ... and I Feel Good!!!!"

See how this can work for you?

And when you are done clarifying, clarify, and clarify some more! Clarify until you can rhyme off exactly what your desire looks like, feels like, smells like, tastes like and sounds like. The natural law of Attraction now has it's "order", just like a catalogue store, outlet or center.

This, or Something Better

Occasionally (and thankfully), we do not get exactly what we stated, and instead, end up with something better! For example, you may have had a mad crush on a certain girl or boy in high school, and were distraught that you just could not get that particular person to pay attention to you. Later on, you found out that in fact, that girl or boy ended up making very bad choices in life, and you are forever thankful that "fate" kept you apart. Law of Attraction works the same way. You can add to your desire thoughts, meditations, goal setting, strategic planning and "A" Statements of all types, "*This, or something better*", as a tag line. *This helps you to detach from exact outcomes, which helps the best results come your way!*

Thank You sincerely!

A Thank You Card

Remember the importance of acknowledgement? Whether in business, personal relationships, or in day to day interactions, a simple "Thank you!" goes a long way. Acknowledgement gets you more of what you are getting … the results you want. The same is true for the natural law of Attraction. Acknowledge to yourself internally, aloud, or even in conversation with others, that something good has occurred, and you will get more of it. Add the following type of thought or statement "Thank You Card" to your Energy System:

With regards to:	Think, Say or Write down this "Thank You Card":
Your main desire or "A" Statement	"I am grateful that Attraction is working for me, orchestrating everything that needs to happen for my _____ to materialize/come true etc ..."
Wanting more abundance in general	Start noticing the abundant resources, people, and things, natural and fabricated, all around you. Think about and comment on these, or begin a journal, listing all your observations.
Good events you don't remember actually giving your attention, energy and focus to	Comment immediately to yourself about the good event, and as soon as possible to an Attraction partner.

Using the "Thank You Card" strategy in your Energy System and acknowledging positive manifestations, will boost your Energy System by strengthening your *Knowing* power.

⊙—ᵐ
Acknowledge to yourself internally, out loud, in writing, or even in conversation with others, that something good has occurred, and you will get more of it.

 Script, and Begin to Create Your Ideal Life

Many years ago, while developing a business venture I was working at for secondary income, I was taught a scripting technique at a motivational seminar. Little did I know at the time, that I was actually learning to apply the law of

Attraction. The technique taught to us was to imagine our perfect day, and to write it all out, in great detail. This seemed difficult to "get started on" at first. But then … it was as if we just could not write fast enough to keep up with our wonderful thoughts.

Remember: Thoughts create things. By thinking in a clear, vivid, positive manner, those things you think about will begin to move towards you.

The script you are writing down today will probably look different from the one you would write down a few months or years from now. Our desires are continually and wonderfully evolving. This is a good thing, and propels us forward to better and better lives.

BA: The rate of change has increased. In business, the strategic plan you develop today is different from that which will be required in as little as one to three years from now.

We are continuously tweaking and stretching our dreams, wants and desires, as we strive for greater joy and personal freedom.

Scripting is a powerful tool to get you into "*Knowing* mode". It will enable your servant brain to work on things you want, without having the "doubt obstacle" in the way. After, all … *you are just pretending, right?* The funny thing about "pretending" is that it is just one more way to give something attention, energy and focus.

Thinking, Imagining, Pretending, Scripting, are all effective Energizers to help you attract more of what you want.

Practice Scripting

Get yourself a special notebook or journal. Make sure it is attractive to you in some way. Perhaps you would prefer a brown leather-bound one, or a colourful dollar store, spiral bound item. Use a pen you enjoy writing with—one that rolls smoothly across the page. The colour of the ink might be special to you. Do your scripting when you can be alone, undisturbed, if at all possible.

Scripting is always an enjoyable activity, and will produce good feelings and vibrations within and around you.

Plan to have about fifteen to twenty minutes to enjoy your scripting time. Pour yourself a delicious cup of tea, fresh water or coffee. Go to a comfortable place in your home or elsewhere, where you feel physically at ease. You may even enjoy this at the coffee shop or library. The next Exercise is a powerful one. You will now write about what your perfect day would be like if you had unlimited health, wealth, time and the ideal relationships and occupations *for you*. Enjoy!

Note: Scripting is an excellent way to "center" yourself and can help in difficult times of illness or turmoil of any type.

Exercise # 13. Scripting Your Perfect Day

Step 1: Close your eyes and take 4 deep and relaxing breaths.

Step 2: Begin by writing in the following style or just fill in the blanks:

I am getting up at _____ (time of day), _____ (alone or with whom), after an excellent and restful sleep. My bedroom _____ (size/location) has_____ _____ (furnishing/features) feels _____ (temperature/describe special features). I enjoy my morning, as I_____ (Describe all the details of your perfect morning. Are you having a luxurious bath or a refreshing shower? What does your beautiful bathroom look like? Include comments about what you or your body look like in your perfect day. What are you wearing? Are you having breakfast? What are you eating? Drinking? Are you exercising? Reading? Watching TV?)
I then go about my day _____ (Describe all your activities and/or ideal Occupation: this should go on for several paragraphs or even pages. Include the vehicle you drive if that is part of your day; include people, places, events you wish for. It could include leisure activities only, or perhaps the perfect career, or maybe sports and the beach. It is whatever makes you feel good to imagine as part of your perfect day.)
My evening is thoroughly enjoyable as I_____ (Describe all the wonderful components of your perfect evening, in great detail, including your meals, bedtime rituals, etc ...

Step 3: Now just relax and complete your activity by taking 4 deep and relaxing breaths.

Note: Scripting your ideal day has many great side effects. One is that if you were having trouble clarifying what desire you wanted to begin working on, to improve your life, you will now have one or two real possibilities to "go for".

<u>Example:</u> If you were fuzzy about what to work on first, and your ideal day has you enjoying a new career instead of the part time job you now have ... well ... Go For It! It is probably time to attract a career switch!

Enjoy your new scripting strategies. Script out your whole life. Yes, your whole life. You may even include your very senior years, in detail, in a scenario whereby you would continue living an active enjoyable life until 100 or 105 years of age, in your own home, with loved ones, and die peacefully in your sleep.

```
          Your personal
     strategic plan ... for
        your whole life!
```

I am in the process of …

Recap Chapter 6: The Power of the Written Word

- The clearer your thinking process is about the things, people and events you want more of, the easier it is for Attraction to bring you more of what you want.

- Acknowledge something good has occurred, and you will get more of it.

- Thinking, Imagining, Pretending, Scripting, are all effective Energizers to help you attract more of what you want.

- In effective "A" Statements, *whatever you are saying,* or even better, *writing down, must feel true, now, to you.*

- "This, or something better." Is a useful Tag Line, promoting detachment and great results!

- Repetition and clarification will Energize your desires. Use describers to clarify your "A" Statements

- Acknowledge positive manifestations

- Script what you want for your entire ideal life

Questions & Ideas

Chapter 7

Be Deliberate and Take Charge of <u>Your</u> Life!

Are You Attracting by Default?

Have you ever wondered how you ended up in a certain situation? Perhaps you have asked yourself "Why me?" Or, have you ever "gotten lucky" and marvelled at your good fortune? *Well, the truth is that you probably brought some or all of it on yourself, the good and the bad.* In fact, we are the primary authors of our fortunes, good or bad. To some extent, we are all "attracting by default". Without the practice of *deliberate* intent, or *deliberate* Attraction, or *deliberate* creation, all manner of "stuff" comes our way, some good, and some bad. We have at some point, attracted at least some of it, by giving it attention, energy and focus.

In case you are still not convinced of this, here are a few common examples.

A.   People who consistently think that finding a parking spot is next to impossible, have really bad "luck" finding a parking spot.

B.   People who say that they get "one really bad cold every year" get one really bad cold (or more!) every year.

C.   People who expect to get fired do.

D.   People who believe they will be single forever, remain that way

E.   People who expect to have travel troubles end up experiencing more delays, baggage loss and rip-offs than others experience.

You have experienced examples of this phenomenon whenever you found yourself saying or feeling, "*I knew this was going to happen!*" You had been repeatedly thinking the event, had *no* doubt about it, and sure enough, it showed up.

Begin re-thinking these scenarios, and ask yourself what would have happened if you and perhaps everyone else involved, would have been thinking something else.

If you do not deliberately intend, and therefore "have a hand" in the creation of the events, people and things that show up in your life, you will continue to, more often than not, attract by default. You may attract some good stuff some of the time, yet you will attract stuff you *do not* want … frequently.

Wouldn't you rather attract a lot more of the good stuff and a lot less of the bad stuff? Wouldn't you want to attract what it is you *truly want*, instead of what you do *not* want?

See what happens next as Andy gives attention, energy and focus to what he *does* want.

Andy & Pam: Before and after deliberately applying Attraction

1. Andy wants his wife Pam to be more relaxed and fun to be around. His thought process looks like this:

"I wish Pam would laugh and joke with me like she used to. She's always grumpy and quiet!"

2. Andy & Pam's conversation usually sounds like this:

"Pam! Why don't you laugh at my jokes?"

"Cause they're not funny! I'm busy...not now..."

3. Andy learns about Attraction. His thought process starts to improve:

"I got a kick out of Pam laughing at that show. Hmmm...she likes that kind of humour...I love those laugh lines she's getting!"

4. Now Andy & Pam's conversation starts to sound like this:

"Do you want to go see a movie this weekend?"

"Let's go see that new Brad Smith comedy."

What About Tornados?

No one is attracting tornados, hurricanes, crashes or other personal and wider scale tragic events of this nature. There are other laws at work in the universe, many of which we do not understand. It is possible that we, as a society or the human race as a massive force, has some type of influence on events, good and bad. This type of dogma is at the basis of every religious or spiritual movement. This possibility is why prayer exists. We must have hope that we can influence outcomes somehow. Hope is part of being human.

It is logical, however, that if a person continuously fears and imagines themselves as having a car accident ... well ... what do *you* think will eventually happen?

You Now Have the Basics of Attraction

There is nothing complicated about applying Attraction to get more of what you want. The law of Attraction works for you, simply by the deliberate application of:

Decide + Energize/*Know*

It is easy, free, and does not require months of course study and training. It all happens between your ears. There are many tools in this book to keep you on track and to assist you in your life improvement plans ... plans that match your core values.

Some of your challenges will come when something you truly desire seems unattainable. The wonderful truth is that it *is* attainable. If any one else on the planet ever achieved a similar goal, then it is possible ... or *you* could be the first. How? You can re-adjust and re-align your thinking, degree by degree, so that you feel better about the availability of your desire. It will move towards you more quickly. What do we mean by this?

At the outset of learning to apply the law of Attraction, you may feel discouragement or doubt about the possibility that you can have, be or do much more of what you truly want. There are strategies to use to overcome these mental obstacles and break free of that unhealthy thinking. Review Chapter 5: *Knowing*. This is probably all you need to get you back on track. If and when you are still finding your desires are not coming easily, the following information will assist you, and ease your transition back into the Healthy Thinking *Attraction* flow of things.

How Is This Happening?

If it is true that if "It" showed up in your life, at some point, you were probably thinking "It" in some form or another, then how can you improve your "chances" of avoiding undesirable events? How can you get better at Attracting the good stuff?

No one wants to attract the bad stuff. No one is purposefully training his or her servant brain to think negatively. People do not set out to sabotage their own lives. What has occurred for people who seem to have a dark cloud over their heads, is that they have allowed themselves to be convinced that bad stuff is always going to come their way, and they may as well just accept it. They have unconsciously patterned their thought processes with fear, low expectations, gloom and all kinds of nastiness about their own lives and possibilities. Their Energy System is programmed to attract negative people, events and circumstances. They have bought into the negative messaging, images and stories they have grown up with, or been exposed to. They may have lived in a dysfunctional family situation. The process may have started at the moment of partnering up with a not-so-Healthy-Thinking boyfriend, girlfriend, or any significant other. It is not easy to pull oneself out of the quicksand of certain situations. *But it can be done … and is done, every single day, all over the planet, by thousands of people.*

What To Do??!?

Take Charge. Period. If you are recognizing yourself in the above scenarios, it is because you have succeeded in attracting a "wake up call" for yourself. Congratulations. It is a message to you that *you do not have to chose the hard and rocky road*. Life can be so much better … so much easier … so much more fun!

You can choose to totally change a difficult situation, a troubled life, a negative life state, by changing your thoughts, one at a time, over and over again. Even those of us who are more adept at Healthy Thinking have to adjust our thought process continuously. We are simply better at reminding ourselves to do it. We are better at fine-tuning and maintaining our Energy System so that it brings us more of the stuff we want, and less of that other stuff. We do end up in negative situations, perhaps through the pull of someone else's agenda. The difference with us is that we use the keys in this book to get back on track … and leave the negative behind.

How? What are you thinking right now? If you stop reading this paragraph and just sit "daydreaming", where do your thoughts go? Where does your mind take you? If your thoughts are automatically taking you to any place that *does not feel good* ... therein lies the problem. Just you realizing this key fact right now, is a positive thing. You are actually self-diagnosing your Attraction "problem".

Note: Relax about any concern you may have about taking charge and attracting something you may regret. There is plenty of time to re-adjust and clarify your desires as you go along. The passage or time between our new desire emerging and the manifestation of it, allows us to revise, tweak, adjust, and even change our mind and work on Attracting something else. This is most evident with our major desires.

Now, try this: start your daydreaming moment again, and the instant your thoughts go somewhere that does not feel good to you, stop, and think of something that feels better. The following table illustrates several examples. It includes a section for you to jot down repetitive unhealthy thoughts you may be having, and healthier thoughts you will now use.

Think Deliberately

If your mind wanders to thoughts of:	*Stop.* Instead think of:
Your illness	What it would feel like to be well again
Your debts	A growing bank balance in your account
A fight you had with your wife	The great sex you had with her last week/month year
Global warming gloom & doom	A new discovery being announced that fuel can be produced pollution free out of household garbage
Your unhappiness at your work	A new job you would like to have
The messy house you have not cleaned	A gift arriving from a friend, for free housecleaning services
<u>Example of a negative or unhealthy repetitive thought you have:</u>	<u>Examples of Healthier thoughts you plan on deliberately thinking from now on:</u>

You get the picture. It does not matter how unrealistic your new Healthier thought is. What matters is that it *feels* better than the one you were thinking. Even one or two "degrees" of feeling better about your thoughts will help tremendously in you taking charge or your own brain! It is *your* mind, *your* brain, *your* thought. You are in control of them. No one else. Partner up with Attraction and make it work *for* you, not against you.

Be Deliberate

Taking Charge of your thinking process is not a mind game. It is the very essence of what successful people do. An old friend of mine, who happens to be a multi-millionaire, used to say that unsuccessful people had "weak minds". Though his comment was somewhat condescending, his observation held merit. Some people, for reasons erroneously thought "out of their control", have unhealthy thinking habits, weak "mind muscles" or poor mind control, to their own detriment.

> Your goal is to begin to *be a Deliberate Attractor/Creator* of your own destiny.

Whether it is to simply lose 10 pounds and get a better job, or become wealthy and move to a different part of the world, it is all the same process.

The key to attracting what you want, or something better, is that
whatever you repeatedly think about,
with simultaneous good feelings, will eventually come to you.
That's it. It is Law. It is irrefutable.
It is at work in every molecule of the Universe.
It is the law of Attraction.

Taking Charge = Intending

Many LOA teachers use the word *intention*, with regards to Taking Charge of what you want, where you want to go, and what you want to do with your life. Entire books are written on the subject of intention. You will enjoy reading these, should you wish to pursue more detail on the subject. In short, intention *is* Taking Charge of your thoughts and *not holding back*. Intention is committing to your desire and simply pointing yourself in that direction.

Taking Charge *Feels* Better

Taking charge of your thinking process will exponentially power up your Energy System. When you control your thoughts, and only *allow negative thought for brief seconds* at a time, you immediately begin to see and feel results, as Attraction gets to work. The first inkling may be just a slight improvement in your mood, or maybe even a "feeling silly" about imagining better things, winnings and special events happening to you. Even that feeling is better than what some people live with their entire lives … a sort of mild discouragement … or even lives of quiet desperation. If you are in that category … you will know what is meant by even the slightest lifting of mood. That wonderful feeling of relief, repeated over and over, can springboard you into a better life. Especially now that you have the tools to keep it going!

About Those Brief Seconds

What is meant by *"only allow negative thought for brief seconds at a time"*? Our servant brain is our most amazing organ. The mind within it, once programmed to think a certain way, has a strong predilection for continuing to operate the same way. Learning a new way takes focus. However … take heart once again! It gets easier.

Strange as this may sound, at first it can be difficult to "hold a positive thought" for even 10 seconds. Try it. Have some fun and test yourself with the "Hold That Thought" Exercise.

Exercise #14. <u>Hold That Thought</u>

<u>Step 1.</u> Choose a positive happy thought, idea, mental picture, phrase, or anything you are comfortable "bringing to mind". Write it down in a few words.

<u>Step 2.</u> Using a watch with a second hand, check the time, close your eyes, and begin thinking your thought.

<u>Step 3.</u> As soon as your mind wanders to another thought, check the time again. Jot down how many seconds you were able to Hold That Thought.

<u>Step 4/Ongoing.</u> Practice this exercise daily and keep a chart to observe your progress in Taking Charge of your Deliberate creation process.

Note: You can choose different thoughts from one day to the next. You should incorporate this type of exercise into your activities of daily living. You can use this Exercise before sleep or upon waking, minus the watch.

"Hold That Thought" Chart	
Day	# of Seconds I was able to Hold The Thought
1	
2	
3	
4	
5	
6	
7	
8	
9	
10	

We have many thousands of thoughts every day. It is impossible to control all of our thoughts. However, it *is* possible to take charge of much of our thinking, apply the natural law of Attraction and take your life in a whole new, healthier and happier direction. Millions have.

Have a Nice Day! ☺

The parting words "Have a Nice Day!" have become as common as "Hello!" There is an inherent message in these words, which we hear so often they can become like auditory wallpaper! Make these words serve as a cue for you to begin living a life where *you* choose what happens next. Simply allow the words to remind you to have an *intentional thought* about the next part of your day. In fact, the choosing of intentional positive thoughts about all the events in your day will trigger good feelings and multiply your positive experiences. Here are some examples of how:

Just before you:	Choose to think about:
Get up in the morning	- what a great day you intend to have. Picture yourself going to bed later that night with a peaceful happy feeling about all the pleasant things that happened today.
Start your work day	- what a good job you will do, and how satisfying that will feel
Begin your daily exercise or workout	- that this workout will strengthen your muscles and burn more fat than usual.
Start your car or get on the train	- what a safe and pleasant journey you will have. Picture yourself leaving the vehicle at your destination, relaxed and refreshed.
Go shopping	- all the savings and great deals you will find.
Make a presentation to a new client	- how impressed the potential client will be, and the orders she will place.
Join a committee meeting	- the great ideas everyone will have and the progress that the group will make

Practicing this type of deliberate, "take charge" thought on a continuous basis will empower you to be the captain of your ship, as opposed to the passenger on someone else's. Enjoy!

Recap Chapter 7: Be Deliberate and Take Charge Of Your Life!

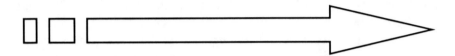

- Your goal is to begin to *be a Deliberate Attractor/Creator* of your own destiny.

- Without the practice of deliberate intent, or deliberate Attraction, or deliberate creation, all manner of "stuff" comes our way, some good, and some bad. We have at some point, attracted it all, by giving it Attention Energy and Focus.

- When you control your thoughts, and only *allow negative thought for brief seconds* at a time, you immediately begin to see and feel results, as Attraction gets to work to bring you good things.

- In fact, the choosing of intentional positive thoughts, about all the events in your day will trigger good feelings and multiply your positive experiences

Questions & Ideas

Chapter 8

Business and Leadership Applications

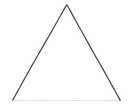

This is no Secret

What is going on in the minds of C-Level executives and Board members? Do you think successful leaders, business owners and millionaires sit around thinking about what they *do not* want? Do you think they mope around, whining about what is *not* working in their organizations? Do you think their thinking process is ineffective, confused and responding to events like a "reed in the wind"?

Applying the elements of the law of Attraction is nothing new to successful business people, nor is it a "secret" to them. They already have the key. They may not have used the term *Attraction*, but they are most certainly operating with the same basic strategies. Many, if not most business leaders have a library of "success oriented" motivational or inspirational reading material, including the exact books mentioned in this one, and many more. Many of them have or are now reading books about the law of Attraction. Some prefer to stay "in the closet" and not reveal the books they are currently reading, especially if there is a perceived "new age" element to the material. The farthest thing from "new age", having been known about for millennia, Attraction's elements are in fact, taught in business school as "basic principles for success", in one form or another.

Whether or not a business or organization chooses to use the terminology of Decide + Energize/*Know*, or even the term "Attraction", is irrelevant. The process for success is the same. To paraphrase Shakespeare, *A rose by any other name is still a rose*. At the very least, all business and service organizations would benefit from the incorporation of the basics of Attraction into their strategic plans and day-to-day operations.

Vision Mission and Values: From So-So to Spectacular

Successful organizations, from small businesses to large corporations, have a basic set of beliefs and desires they operate from, whether they have ever actually written these down or not. These unfortunately, have a significant "yawn factor" for the majority of their employees, and often, no one ever really pays any attention to these, once crafted. Sadly, a key tool for organizational development and success is being left on the shelf.

Conversely, once everyone "gets it" about the Vision Mission and Values, they will "buy in" and *feel good* about these, creating pride of membership *feelings* in their place of work. We all know the bottom line results *that* feeling produces.

The Big Three: "VMV"

For our purposes, consider the following definitions for these well-worn terms:

<u>Vision:</u> Whatever your organization would like to see in an "ideal world", where resources and time are abundant. If everything were perfect, what would be the scenario? What would your organization have accomplished?

<u>Mission:</u> What your organization's "job" is. What the organization is funded or paid for, whether through government funding, charitable intake or sales revenues.

<u>Values:</u> Your organization's beliefs. The concepts and philosophy that everyone should be working with and practicing.

The Key is in the Vision

Visit the web sites of the world's most powerful and successful corporations. Read their Vision statements. Bar none, they are crafted to elicit a *feeling*. A strong, clear Vision statement will work the same way as the Decide step in attracting the desired results. Remember: either you can choose to pilot your ship with a clear course, or you can be a passenger on someone else's. Your Vision statement guides your organization in the right direction.

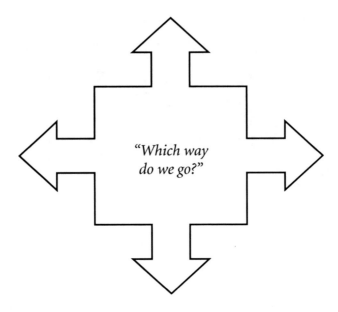

"Which way do we go?"

A good Vision Mission Values "piece" elicits *good feelings*. It should make people feel better about associating with the company. Successful organizations know that this "feeling stuff" is so important to the success of their business, or to the achievement of their goals, that huge amounts of money are spent on creating "Vision Mission Values" statements. These statements are not only meant to clarify what they are about, these are intended to get people to "bond with the company", "buy in" or even "get all fired up". *That feeling is what attracts the desired results.*

The Leader Should Lead

Job One for the person in the corner office, the entrepreneur launching a one-person new enterprise, and for the head of every department, is to get everyone in alignment with the Vision, Mission and Values, but most importantly, the Vision. The leader should have the skills to work with others in the organization to develop the Vision and *attract* the resources to *make it so*. For organizations which are currently dysfunctional, at a very minimum, while developing a healthier organization, the leader must have her or his organizational Vision clearly defined for themselves. The Exercises in all previous Chapters are applicable for any CEO, Administrator, Manager or Entrepreneur. They can also be easily adapted for use in group settings for planned organizational development. The following is an example of Attraction at work on a complex Vision project.

Groupthink

Attempts at organizational change, as well as basic system development, can be sabotaged by Groupthink. If 100% of the people involved continue to think negative, cynical, discouraged thoughts, positive change *cannot* occur. Groups of people thinking a particular thought is, unfortunately, powerful indeed. Remember: thoughts create things. The solution to this problem, in existence since we began to think for ourselves, is to "turn the ship around". *It takes one captain, and a small group of like-minded individuals to change the course from a dangerously negative one, to a hopeful, positive, sustainable and successful one.* Do your own research on organizational change and development, and you will find many examples of this process at work. My favourite example is that of the now world famous FISH™ philosophy. Form it's inception at Seattle's Pike Place Fish Market™, to boardrooms and staff lounges of organizations world wide, big and small, this simple strategy has positively changed countless workplaces.

"Be There, Play, Make Their Day and Choose Your Attitude™" is the simple path "FISH" leaders take to attract and foster Healthy Thinking and organizational health to their companies.

I have been fortunate enough to work in a company where the Executive Director had decided to implement the FISH™ philosophy, in an organization not particularly known for being a "fun" place to work. The change was phenomenal, to the ultimate benefit of the client.

What is Your Company's Vision?

Do you know exactly what it is you are trying to achieve now, with your company? Are you attracting that, or something else, by default? Decide what your Vision is, start putting some attention, energy and focus (Energize) behind that Decision, and enjoy the results.

Here are some practical examples where this is of key importance, as well as some suggestions for process.

Setting	Vision Process
New business venture	Spend one day thinking about your Vision, and putting some words to it. Try it on for size using sheets of paper on your office walls. Sleep on it … what does it look like to you the next morning? Will the client be attracted to your product or service? Will your Vision inspire you and your partners or employees?
Large organization where major change is required	Have your staff answer the following question in an email or anonymous suggestion box: "In a perfect world, where resources and time is abundant, what do you see our company doing or being?"
Small business or charitable organization operating with no actual publicized Vision	Spend a day working through the question above, creating, revising and constructing your Vision statement. It should be one that everyone would be proud to tell people about. This will have many positive side effects including team building as well as boosting ownership and accountability feelings within staff.

Once you and your company have a strong, clear inspirational Vision, your Mission and Values will be simpler to craft. Next, you will find the development of your Strategic, Business and Operational Plans will flow, enabling you to more easily enlist the partnership of financing and funding bodies as well as the right people to make it all happen at the front lines.

Applying the Basic Formula

How do you create a successful business using Attraction? Simply by following the same process you will follow for your personal life. Remember, it is still people … individuals with thinking minds, and desires of their own, who are expected to create success in the business. The process remains: the key to attracting what you want, is that *whatever you repeatedly think about, with simultaneous good feelings, will eventually come to you.* And so, if you are serious about creating a successful business, know that the application of that same Attraction principle will make you and your organization unstoppable.

The following template will guide you and your organization in this process:

Attraction Template for Businesses and Organizations

Healthy Thinking	Work with your administration and management group to minimize, and eventually eliminate, Problem Words being currently used in your organization's meeting rooms, offices, documents and publicized materials.

Decide	A. Identify all the problem areas in your organization, the "things you don't want", or all the areas needing improvement. Create this list with your leaders first. Together, you can then work with the front line staff, using the same process.
	Remember: someone has to pilot the ship.
	B. Model and encourage everyone to start talking about what they *do* want.
	C. Use a standard strategic planning exercise to now Decide on the main Goals for your business or organization.

Energize	A. Apply Energy Attention and Focus to the organization's strategic goals, using as many of the senses as possible.
	For Example:
	Visual: new advertising, use of your new Vision statement everywhere, new logos, and paint colours, creative use of media and promotional material. *Visual cues are powerful.*
	Auditory: Use of music appropriate for your business, as cues, matching your Vision and the message you are promoting. Use it in waiting rooms, bathrooms, elevators, meetings.
	Tactile: Renovations to facilities, improved seating and flooring, temperature control, exercise facilities. In-servicing and training for front line staff performing any work, which actually involves human contact, be it shaking hands or health care procedures: the goal is to match the skill and style of touch used to the organization's Vision.

Energize	_Scent:_ eliminate scent or use the appropriate scent to match the Vision and type of organization. _Taste:_ Review and improvement of all ingested fluids and foods available in the organization, to match these to the Vision and goals where possible. Provide and offer healthy refreshments to clients. **B.** Initiate action in the direction of each of your strategic plan's goals or strategies, while _Knowing_ you will succeed, and achieve these, or something better. For Example:<ul><li>Do The Tough Stuff First: apply new ideas and move in new directions, from decisions which are evidence-based wherever possible. Certain initiatives can be radical or unpopular with some who are more resistant to change</li><li>Seek out new funding sources you may have hesitated to approach previously</li><li>Explore new partnerships, alliances and collaborations with like-minded groups an business peers</li><li>Hire and/or promote positive thinkers, people who are able to think differently from the majority, while engaging in your Vision</li><li>Bring in new "non task related" learning activities for your managers, enabling them to boost their own leadership capacity</li><li>Seek out the leaders within the front lines, and enlist their energy</li><li>Approach new client bases and develop new alliances for improved service, using new and even radical techniques</li></ul>

Know	- In meetings or conversations with managers and employees, use factual anecdotes and stories about other similar type or size organizations who have achieved similar goals. - With new one-owner/one worker business enterprises, use the same strategy as part of your own Attraction process to grow your business.

| Know | - Express gratitude and appreciation, for real events and results, with all those involved in your organization.
- Acknowledge clients for entrusting their needs to you.
- Celebrate events and small successes which move the organization towards the Vision. |

Review and renew all the above quarterly, with all involved, and re-adjust as required.

Use the Basics to Change the Culture of Your Organization

Once you have a Vision for your new business or existing organization, it is much simpler to begin to change and improve the culture, should that be required. Unfortunately, with the pace and rate of change everyone is subjected to, most places have a certain level of negativity which threaten to keep the "what we *don't* want" issues at the forefront of people's minds, perpetuating problems.

The following are some basic tips to get you and your organization redirected, day-to-day, in order to get more of what you want, and less of what you do not want.

Fundamental Change

From the boardroom, to the top levels of administration and throughout the workplace, be alert to conversations and meetings turning to complaints or repetitive "broken record" comments about seemingly unsolvable problems. *It takes is one person* to ask the following question, and get the Energy shifted to finding solutions.

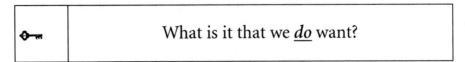

What is it that we *do* want?

In the development of successful healthy organizations, the same concept applies. "*Hire for Attitude—Train for Skill*" has taken many a workplace from dismal and dysfunctional to leaders in their field. Leaders, small business entrepreneurs and human resources managers who are successful in attracting the right people to their organizations, do so by maintaining focus on the right kinds of people for the positions available. They purposefully want and focus on attracting only those who are like-minded, demonstrate positive attitudes in interviews, and can produce proof of this quality with strong references. The ability to develop teams, which are comfortable imagining and discussing the *possibilities* for their work, and to *know the Vision can be a reality,* is organizational development magic.

Hiring staff with the right healthy attitude will prepare and take your organization through hard times, and contribute greatly to the achievement of your goals.

> ◘━ It is better to hire a positive thinking person, with the basic core skills you require for the job, and train them for the more complex work required, than it is to hire the super-skilled PhD level candidate carrying a grudge and an attitude of entitlement to the workplace every day.

Review the Chapter 2 on Healthy Thinking, and apply the same basic ideas to get yourself and your employees thinking in a manner that is effective for the achievement of the goals your organization has set. There is a monumental difference between organizations where a positive healthy attitude prevails, and those where gloom, doom and cynicism are the modus operandi.

- Which do you want for your business?
- Which do you think will improve the service goals and bottom line of your organization?
- Which will attract and satisfy the client, the shareholder or the Board member?

What do we Decide to Attract First?

Organizations can apply the Big FOHR described in Chapter 4: Energize to refocus efforts and resources on clear goals you may have thought were previously unattainable. The Decide step launches the goals you have for your business, and enlists the law of Attraction as your "top employee", working for you 24/7, 365.

You may have so many things and situations in your life or your business that you want to change, that you feel overwhelmed. However, the changes you want will begin to take place, just as you intend, by adapting and applying the tools in this book.

The *Attraction Template for Businesses and Organizations* outlines the Decide step and its application in the business realm. *Using the same strategies* you would for yourself in your personal life, you and your organization can determine the outcomes you wish to attract. In fact, a simple use of these strategies can help any manager or leader to walk her organization through the goal-setting component of Strategic Planning ... and save yourself some expenditure on consultant fees! You could even develop a few in-house experts to become your own strategic planning crew, and create leadership within the ranks.

<u>The Big FOHR</u>

Finances
Occupation
Health
Relationships

Finances

Decide on the financial, sales, investment and growth goals for the organization. This list can be further developed into sub categories by department, or other criteria appropriate to your field. Remember to encourage your employees, managers, and each other, to aim high. The One Big Wish strategy described in Chapter 3: Decide, can easily be adapted and applied in a group workshop for your decision-making.

Examples of the One Big Wish your organization may come up with:

1.   The entrepreneur's fledgling one-person business: <u>earn a 6-figure income</u> to independently support his family

2.   The 20-employee real estate company: <u>double their sales</u> in one year

3.   The newly launched foundation for support of the independent elderly: <u>meet the needs of 1000 frail elderly</u> who wish to stay in their own homes

4.   The internet retail sales outlet: <u>become the consumer's number one choice</u> in 6 months

Occupation

What are your organization's main occupation-related goals? Management and Human Resource departments grapple with these every day. Is there one area that challenges your potential progress? Is there one main issue that could potentially sabotage your efforts? Is there one problem that, once solved, would catapult you into a more successful future?

Examples of the One Big Wish your organization may come up with:

1.   The large governmental organization paralyzed by bureaucracy: <u>simplify</u> the organization's structure and processes in order to double productivity and better serve the people

2.   The health care organization facing major staffing shortages: <u>be the model/magnet</u> organization in the area

3.   The small service business: <u>find one highly skilled team leader</u>

4.   The church group: build and maintain <u>a committed group of volunteers</u>

<u>Health</u>

What are the main health-related issues your organization needs to address? Evidence now shows that ignoring these issues and acting as if the organization as an entity has no responsibility toward employees' health, is counterproductive. Addressing and making progress in even one area of individual employee health can make a big difference. Companies who rank in the "most favoured to work for" take employee health seriously, to everyone's benefit, and to the benefit of the bottom line.

Examples of the One Big Wish your organization may come up with:

1.   The construction company: work 365 days <u>without any lost time injury</u>

2.   The telemarketing company: enable all staff to <u>become smoke-free</u>

3.   The restaurant: <u>win</u> public health healthy eating <u>awards</u> 5 years in a row

4.   The banking conglomerate: the <u>best employee wellness and attendance record</u> in the industry

Relationships

This one comes easy to any business involved in sales or direct customer service: put the client first. The client/customer/patient/buyer's satisfaction is at the center of the company's number one goal. With even just one competitor, should the client not be satisfied, he or she will simply go across the street, or to another website, and spend their hard-earned money there.

Examples of the One Big Wish your organization may come up with:

1.   The health care organization: <u>patients</u> consistently report they <u>feel their needs are the organization's number one priority</u>

2.   The investment group: <u>clients will remain</u> with the company through their life span

3.   The school: <u>parents and children will report they feel happy, satisfied and proud</u> to belong to the school

4.   The travel agency: <u>clients will book with the agency year after year</u> and refer others to us

Ask One Question

Applying the basic principles of Attraction to the existing day-to-day operations of your organization *will* yield results. You may have some doubters or negative reactions initially. However, organizations which have implemented these tried and true positive thinking, results-oriented methods would never go back to the way it was. Change must come from the top down. However, if you are not in a leadership position and feel you want to trigger positive change, remember …

It only takes one person to ask …

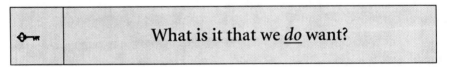

What is it that we _do_ want?

… and watch what happens.

Proof Notes: Attraction in Action

Whether in the front lines or in leadership positions, I have been on many teams in the course of my career. From the powerful vision of one or more leaders, through many challenges, opposing forces and sometimes "from zero resources", here are a few examples of manifestations I have been a part of, which were classic "Attraction in action":

- the building of a new hospital
- the accumulation of cash reserves far beyond those of other peer organizations
- the creation of a new community college
- the construction of a new nursing home
- the launch of an innovative health care community center
- the implementation of healthy workplace philosophies
- transforming service from local to international programming
- the creation of multiple & diverse sources of income
- the amassing of real estate required to achieve growth goals
- the launch of the first computerized electronic "e-mail-able X Ray" system in our large geographical area
- the successful implementation of the first "a laptop for every student" program in our organizational peer group … and everyone said it couldn't be done … it is now the norm

These are just a few examples I have experienced or been a part of, where the power of Decide, Energize and *Know* triggered the elements of Attraction in the organizational and business world. There is no question in my mind that the process is the same, though termed in varying and more complex ways … someone, somewhere, is unwavering in applying their attention, energy and focus to the Vision. There is much to be done … and there are many dedicating their lives right now, in the corporate, not-for-profit and entrepreneurial world … to *doing good things with what they know*.

Questions & Answers

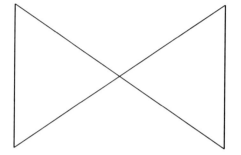

For Enquiring Minds

The basic elements of Attraction are presented to you in this book, enabling you to immediately apply these. You will probably have a new thirst for knowledge on the subject, and I hope the following answers will help. As previously stated, there is a library of information on the subject, and a growing number of teachers, guides and mentors ready to inspire you further, and to take you Beyond Positive Thinking. Enjoy!

This section of common Questions and Answers is intended to shed further light on, and clarify various elements of Attraction.

Please forward new Questions to questions@youattractnow.com

1. "Do I have to believe in Attraction for it to work?"

No. Attraction does not care if you believe in it or not. It is a natural universal law, and works for everyone. You are already using it: it is always at work in your life. You get more of what you Decide & Energize while *Knowing*. Period.

2. "I work in a very negative workplace. How can I stay positive?"

The more positive you become, even in a negative environment, the more you will attract positive people, events and circumstances, even in a nasty workplace. Something to think about for you: are you in a workplace that does not match what you are all about? Should you be thinking about attracting a career move? People everywhere do it every day.

3. "My spouse thinks I'm crazy and won't listen to me talk about Attraction. What should I do?"

Be yourself. Continue applying Attraction. Stay positive. Acknowledge the nice things your spouse is saying and doing, with a heartfelt "thank you". It is not your job to convert anyone. Your spouse will no doubt enjoy and reap the benefits of Attraction in your lives. His or her perspective may eventually change. Regardless of your spouse's reaction, *you* will get less of what you *do not* want, and more of what you *do* want.

4. "I'm doing the Decide, Energize/*Know*, and I still don't have my desire. What am I doing wrong?"

First, re-check your *Knowing* strategies. Are you ensuring that you are getting good feelings, *really good feelings,* when you are thinking about the things you want? Doubt will cancel out your desire every time—get good at the Knowing part and Attraction gets into high gear.

Secondly, remember, there is a time factor—a safety cushion to protect you from "getting" everything you think about immediately.

Thirdly: Would the manifesting of your wish directly harm another individual? If so, a deep desire within you to "do good, or to do the right thing" may be cancelling out your current wish.

5. "I have trouble visualizing my desire, because I just can't picture it actually coming true for me."

Use the "road" technique described in Chapter 4: Energize, True Love Proof Notes. Picture your desire *on a road, river or train on its way to you.* That will allow your mind to accept and *Know* that it *is* in fact possible. It is simply on its way, that's all. Or you may try the scrolling of your desire in word or phrase form in your mind, like a screen saver.

Remember: your way of visualizing may be different than someone else's … whatever works for you is perfect!

6. "Does this law of Attraction information contradict my religion?"

No. The natural law of Attraction is *not* God. The Higher Power, regardless of the name you and your particular belief system has given it, is infinitely more powerful than any one of the natural laws. Attraction is simply one natural law, just as Gravity is. Religion and all manner of organized spiritual practices already incorporate elements of this law, in varying forms, using different vocabulary. The renewed interest in this "*thinking creates your reality*" fact, should have no more impact on religious practices than did the discovery that the world was round, and not flat. The natural law of Attraction is being used everywhere, by people of all faiths, right now, to do good in the world … whether they realize it or not. Increased awareness and deliberate application of Attraction can and will create more good on our planet.

7. "I still find myself thinking negatively some of the time. What if I am not practicing Healthy Thinking all the time?"

Well, congratulations! You are human after all. No one is able to maintain any type of exactly perfectly organized thought 100% of the time. This is why tools like the Exercises in this book are necessary for the continuous improvement to the Health of our thinking process. And that goes for every single one of us.

8. "If this law of Attraction is as everyone says it is, and Decide Energize/*Know* will enable you to get more of what you want, then why isn't every one winning the lottery?"

There are several reasons for any desire not yet manifesting. <u>First</u>, it is in the *Knowing* element that we usually encounter the obstacles. Even skilled practitioners of deliberate creation through Attraction have areas where deep down, they have not convinced themselves that a certain desire is on the way ... *yet*. <u>Secondly</u>, many people are not interested in winning the lottery, and are putting their attention energy and focus on different desires. <u>Thirdly</u>, the time between the Deciding and the manifesting of any given desire varies, thankfully! Having every single thing we think we want at every moment would be total chaos. <u>Also,</u> millions and millions of people are focusing their attention and energy on winning *the same lottery*. There is only one or a few winners each time. The winnings always go to those who, deep down, just *knew* their desire was on its way.

9. "I am really applying the 2 steps (Decide & Energize) as well as *Knowing*, to a major problem in my work place, but seem to be getting nowhere. Those who are perpetuating the problem have all the power and I feel like nothing will ever change. What else can I do?"

Remember that whether consciously or not, everyone, including the perpetrators of the problem, is already attracting things, people and events to their lives. You are not responsible for what others are attracting to themselves. You can continue using deliberate Attraction strategies, yet you may want to re-direct them to the eventual Attraction of new like-minded people to your workplace. Going to the "dark side" and giving in, is not in alignment with who you are in this realm of your world. Have you explored the possibility that this work place experience is no longer a match for you? Is it possible that you need to attract an exciting new career path, or perhaps a transfer to a new department? The possibilities are endless.

10. "Will I be lumped in with the crystal and incense people?"

Only if that is something that interests you, and you choose those activities. Remember … Attraction works for everyone, everywhere, all the time. That includes the crystal and incense people. World leaders, business people, scientists, philosophers and psychologists, cashiers, moms and even children are deliberately applying the natural law of Attraction right now … to their benefit.

11. "Isn't this Attraction stuff simply us becoming biased and finding what we are looking for?"

You are talking about *Confirmation Bias Theory*. In scientific trials, when the researcher has an un-checked bias about the eventual result (she or he *wants* the result to be "x", and there is nothing built into the research process to ensure this does not happen), the findings can be inaccurately skewed to that desired result. There are mountains of evidence, since history was recorded, of the natural law of Attraction at work, whether you believe it or not, whether biases were at play or not. We simply get more of what we think about, especially when we have strong feelings about the thought … period.

12. "We just had a death in our family. How can we even think one positive thought when we are all grieving?"

Grieving is a natural part of our human existence. However, it is possible to think more positive thoughts, while grieving. Those are the wonderful memories you hold of the loved one you have lost. Over time, those memories take the lead in your mind, and the feeling of excruciatingly painful grief recedes, as nature intends. In the meantime, it is wise to make an effort to bring forward as often as possible, those happier, sweeter, positive memories of your loved one. It will help to avoid focus on the tragedy of the death itself, the suffering the person may have endured, or any painful circumstances surrounding the death. Focus on the fond memories. Remaining stuck in any of the natural stages of grief can hold you back in many ways. Get connected with friends and loved ones who can help you re-focus, remember the good times, and plan positive activities.

13. "I prefer to ask my Higher Power for things I need. How can I apply Attraction as well?"

You are, in fact, already applying one of the elements of Attraction, by asking your Higher Power for what you need. *Deciding* and *asking* serve the same function. Whether you are following rituals of organized religion, such as praying, or live your life as an agnostic, the natural law of Attraction works the same way. Review Chapter 3: Decide, for further clarification.

14. "I have tried 7-step techniques, meditating during my work breaks, and a variety of other popular business strategies to try to boost sales. I am still treading water. What should I change?"

Many successful people, in sports, business and other fields, including myself, do not use complex multi-step systems for success. Many of us do not stop the flow of action, to meditate mid-stream. These ideas are admittedly useful, do have excellent tips and great principles embedded within, and do help millions of people. They are especially useful to get someone started in new initiatives. However, I have found that in day-to-day practice, many of these are simply too complex, and in the crunch of a moment, successful people make important actions and decisions seemingly by instinct ... the instinct of *Knowing*. They just keep going and going, *Knowing* they will succeed, and adjusting plans as required. Attraction, and other forces at work in the successful mind then manifest the desire ... or something better. Most CEOs I have worked with have an obvious, or a well-camouflaged trait some would term "a rebellious streak". Regardless of what others think, they Know they are on the right track, do the tough stuff first, and press on, while adjusting and tweaking their "plan" as required.

15. "How can I teach my children these concepts?"

Easily. Children will do what you do. Though they will grow into their own unique personalities and have interests different from yours, they cannot help but live what they learn at their parents' side, and in the family home. Even when you do not feel like it, try to remember the basic steps and apply them yourself, to a Decision about the way you want your children to be: happy, learning, respectful, preparing to be independent adults able to learn from mistakes and make a contribution to the world. Stay positive; show them Healthy Thinking, using age-appropriate language. You will be able to teach them the actual process of Decide + Energize/*Know*, just as it is in this book, when you feel they are ready. For some that can be as early as four or five. They can use the strategies to move away from what feels bad to them, and move towards good things, events and people. Let them have fun with it. Help them make a Dream Board. The possibilities are endless.

A Different Kind of Conclusion

> *It is not possible to solve a problem within the same consciousness that produced it.*
> Albert Einstein

The keys are in your hands, or rather *in your mind*. Being more, having something different or simply more of it, and doing what you really want to do, are all possible for you. Life improvements have always have been within your grasp. Thinking in healthy, productive, enriching ways will always yield better outcomes than the alternative. Going beyond positive thinking, to deliberately attracting your desires, is your right, your gift, your well-deserved reward, and sometimes even ... your responsibility. *You will understand what I mean by responsibility when you read the final page of this conclusion. The power of Attraction can do much more than simply draw new things into our lives.*

Many books will provide you further, more elaborate detail on the law of Attraction, and other variations on this, one of the most important laws at work in our world. The body of knowledge on the subject is now in a mode of expansion never before seen. You are now part of this phenomenon, though I am sure that many of the ideas presented in this book were familiar to you, since, as stated early on ... the law of Attraction is already and always at work in your life right now. Though the knowledge of how to use the keys and apply Attraction deliberately is within all of us, until we master this knowledge and apply it automatically, we need "how-to's" and reminders ... this book, your manual, is full of them. Use these ideas, exercises and keys daily, and the results will cause you to wonder how you ever managed before this.

You have keys in your hands, within the pages of this book, which you can use as is, or adapt to your circumstances and needs. The 2-step formula of Decide + Energize, all the while *Knowing* you will obtain your desired result "or something better", is simply the most user-friendly explanation of the Law Of

Attraction and its application you will ever find. Exercises and information have been kept easy and enjoyable, yet many of them are adaptable for group work in any organization. You can start today, to bring towards you exactly the kind of life you desire. Though many books are written on matters of success, it is my hope that you now have a clearer, simpler direction to follow, and some easy to understand "how-to" information so that *you* can move forward, regardless of where life finds you at this very moment.

Thirsty for more? Start with some of the treasures in the "References & Suggested Readings" section at the back of this book, and build your own Attraction library. Visit www.youattractnow.com for more resources and as your place to find further inspiration and information.

Now press on, enjoy your newfound riches and remember, *"There is always something to look forward to."*

À la prochaine … until the next time … Gisèle.

<u>We Can Change The World ... One Minute At A Time.</u>

There is one more thing I must say, a thing that is far Beyond Positive Thinking.

How would you like to have an impact on the world, and help reverse global warming, or educate and feed the developing nations? How about improving access to wealth and resources, for the poor in our own countries? Perhaps you would like to have a positive influence on the status of a particular group, such as women, or migrant workers, or orphaned children.

We *can* influence these issues and make a difference. We can reverse global warming and positively influence all of the above issues and any others that you can think of. How? By thinking. The same process discussed throughout this book, Decide + Energize/Know can be applied to any issue. Imagine the possibilities if massive numbers of us applied the law of Attraction to the reversal of global warming. Imagine if we applied the process and systematically, little by little, we moved in *that* direction. The impact would be staggering ... positively massive.

I am encouraging all of you to choose an issue, and start talking to others about making it a habit to spend one minute each day, applying attention, energy and focus to the solution required and to share the following with others:

<u>I am calling upon everyone who reads this book,</u>
<u>to spend one minute each day, from now on, *imagining* the following:</u>

There is peace throughout the planet.
The air all across the globe is pure, fresh and clean.
The waters flowing through our lakes, rivers and oceans is crystal clear and carries only the natural elements and life it was intended to hold.
The soil under our feet, everywhere, in every country, is alive with natural nutrients, and life springs freely from its bountiful depths.
The creatures of the earth abound in glorious diversity and great numbers.
Healthy, sustainable processes are now in use, for all our needs,
including energy and fuel, food production,
and all manner of required consumables.
The human race has turned massive knowledge and resources towards the health of the planet, and people everywhere are *doing good with what we know.*

Now begin each day, to move in the direction of this vision.

References & Suggested Readings

Behrend, Genevieve *Your Invisible Power: The Mental Science of Thomas Troward* De Vorss & Company 1951

Chopra, Deepak (M.D.) *Creating Affluence* New World Library 1993

Dyer, Dr. Wayne *The Power of Intention* Hay House, Inc., 2004

Dyer, Dr Wayne *You'll See It When You Believe It* Avon Books 1990
Einstein, Albert *The World As I See It*, Copyrighted essay originally published in Forum and Century 1931
Hill, Napoleon *You Can Work Your Own Miracles* Fawcett Publications 1971

James, William *Principles of Psychology* Harvard 1890

Losier, Michael J., *Law of Attraction* Losier 2006

Murphy, Dr. Joseph, *The Power of Your Subconscious Mind*, Prentice-Hall 1963

Nightingale, Earl *The Strangest Secret* Nightingale Conant (First publication 1957)

Peale, Norman Vincent Peale *The Power of Positive Thinking* (First publication 1952) Fawcett Publications 1990

Ponder, Catherine *The Dynamic Laws of Prosperity* (First publication 1962) De Vorss & Company 1993

Towne, Elizabeth *15 Lessons in New Thought or Lessons in Living* (Essay publication/Self 1910)

Varia/Media

Byrne, Rhonda et al The Secret (DVD Movie): see www.thesecret.tv

The FISH! Philosophy®: find it at ChartHouse Learning® www.charthouse.com

Nightingale, Earl *The Strangest Secret* First recording 1956, (currently on CD) Nightingale Conant

About the Author

Gisèle Guénard holds a Bachelor of Science/Nursing degree from Laurentian University, as well as a Master of Education degree from the University of Toronto. Always writing, she worked her way up the leadership ladder while raising two daughters, now happy, married and successful in their own careers. Gisèle has held positions as a Registered Nurse, Team Leader, College Professor, Administration Coordinator, Manager of Education, Director of Clinical Services and Chief Executive Officer. She has held various committee leadership positions in the province of Ontario, Canada, worked on the development of nursing licensure examinations, and has written a nursing textbook in the French language.

Along the way, Gisèle has inspired thousands to move towards their personal and organizational goals, and to *do good things with what they know*. From her work caring for countless hospital patients, families and communities, to inspiring nursing students, to her leadership and vision in the health care system, Gisèle's message has remained constant. She has faced many personal tragedies including the death of many beloved friends and family members, as well as countless marvelous experiences and always … moved through her life's work with an attitude *Beyond Positive Thinking*.

An avid reader since early childhood, Gisèle's knowledge and understanding of the keys to success have continuously expanded and become the center of her work. The writing of *Attract It: Beyond Positive Thinking* was a journey triggered by the passing of her beloved Mother, a true spirit of goodness and light. The crystallizing of time-honored success concepts, including the law of Attraction, into her simple, 2-step, <u>Decide + Energize/*Know*</u> system, is typical of Gisèle's well-known skill at "saying the words" that need to be said. Gisèle believes that leaders have a responsibility to share the basics of positive thinking, and use their influence to literally *change the world*. Hence, *The Manual*.

Gisèle enjoys a fulfilling life, rich with diverse activities, in Ontario, Canada. She and her equally musical husband John enjoy entertaining at gatherings of all sorts, be they urban, or be they magical Boréal forest waterfront.

978-0-595-43377-3
0-595-43377-4

Printed in the United States
99417LV00003B/271-369/A